lead yourself

BE WHO
AND WHAT
TO

YOU ARE
YOU WANT
BE

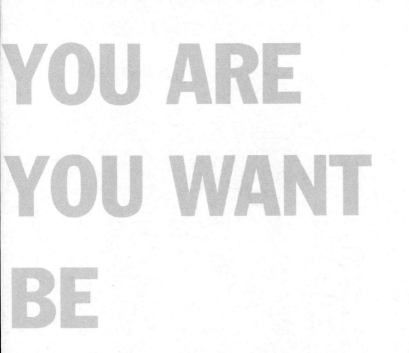

lead yourself

be who you are and what you want to be

second edition

Mick Cope

www.yourmomentum.com
the stuff that drives you

What is momentum?

Momentum is for people who want to make things happen in their career and their life, who want to work at something they enjoy and that's worthy of their talent and their time. Momentum people have values and principles and question who they are, what they do, and who for. Wherever they work, they want to feel proud of what they do. And they are hungry for information, stimulation, ideas and answers.

More momentum

If you need more drive for your life, try one of these other momentum titles:

change activist 2e
make big things happen fast
Carmel McConnell

coach yourself 2e
make real change in your life
Anthony M. Grant and Jane Greene

PEARSON EDUCATION LIMITED

Edinburgh Gate
Harlow CM20 2JE
Tel: +44 (0)1279 623623
Fax: +44 (0)1279 431059
Website: www.pearsoned.co.uk

First published 2003
Second edition published in Great Britain in 2006

© Pearson Education Limited 2003, 2006

ISBN-13: 978-0-273-70784-4
ISBN-10: 0-273-70784-1

British Library Cataloguing in Publication Data
A catalogue record for this book can be obtained from the British Library

Library of Congress Cataloging-in-Publication Data

Cope, Mick.
    Lead yourself : before leading others : be who you are and what you want to be / Mick Cope. – 2nd ed.
    p. cm.
    Includes bibliographical references and index.
    ISBN-13: 978-0-273-70784-4 (pbk.)
    ISBN-10: 0-273-70784-1 (pbk.)
    1. Leadership. 2. Self-actualization (Psychology) I. Title.

BF637.L4C58 2006
158'.4—dc22
                                    2006044850

10 9 8 7 6 5 4 3 2 1
10 09 08 07 06

Cover design by Heat
Text design by Claire Brodmann Book Designs, Lichfield, Staffs
Typeset in 10/14pt Palatino by 70
Printed in Great Britain by Henry Ling Ltd, at the Dorset Press, Dorchester, Dorset

The publisher's policy is to use paper manufactured from sustainable forests.

dedication

for Lin, Mike, Joe and Lucy – the loves of my life

thank you ...

to all who have helped with my journey. Also big thanks to Christine Blanshard and Marc Baker for helping tidy the book and the ideas, and Janice and Tony Hansford for helping us to be what we want to be.

contents

contents

about the author

Mick Cope is MD of WizOz Ltd a network organization that seeks to help people and businesses optimize their potential. He has three roles in his professional life: as a consultant, author and Head of WizOz Ltd. As an author he has published seven books to date: *Leading the Organisation to Learn; The Seven Cs of Consulting; Know your value? Value what you know; Lead Yourself; Float You; Personal Networking* and *The Seven Cs of Coaching.*

He is always really keen to discuss his ideas with people – so feel free to email him at mick@mickcope.com.

introduction

THINK OF the people in life who just knock you out. The ones who, when you meet them, have purpose, passion and persistence. They are able to set a direction and follow through without fear of what others might say or what the world might think. These people don't do this because their boss says it is in the job description; because they need to impress someone or as the result of a New Year's resolution. They steer a clear direction for themselves and others because it is the right thing to do; and by having such clarity of purpose they are able to make the right choices and help bring other people on board for the journey.

It may be that you find yourself in a position where you are fed up at work but cannot think of anything better to do, you might have a dream but are too scared to take the first step, or you might be faced with a range of choices and cannot see how to pick the one that will help you achieve your goals. This is where the personal leadership framework comes in. It introduces a range of simple tools and techniques that help you to be who you are and what you want to be.

By developing such personal rather than plastic leadership you will be able to find your own purpose in life, make the choices that help deliver the purpose, overcome those deep hidden doubts and delusions that hinder progress and bring others on board to help deliver your goal.

However, personal leadership isn't something you get from the back of a cereal box or off a bookshelf. This book will help you think about how you might make improvements, differing ways to approach a situation and how to understand other people's leadership preferences. The key thing is that the book can only ever offer ideas – it can never offer solutions. Personal leadership is just that – it is personal, and as such the journey is a private one.

The choices you make (or don't make) are the single most important element of leading yourself or others. But choice is often the thing that we think least about, and we are rarely taught how to use it with real focus and wisdom.

From a young age, many of us fall into the trap of thinking we don't own the choices we make. We use phrases such as 'they made me do it', 'I can't help saying that', or 'it was my parents' fault'. True – these may well have influenced the way that choices are made – but this doesn't mean that we don't have the ability to change those choices. The essence of leading yourself and others lies in understanding the choices you make and then being prepared to learn how to change them. By taking this first step it becomes possible to truly develop how you lead yourself, and in due course lead others.

Personal leadership choices

Regardless of whether you're a parent, manager, aspiring career climber or student, there are six core choices that influence how we lead ourselves and others:

1 how we actually make choices;

2 how we set direction;

3 how we discard false assumptions;

4 how we become more adaptive;

5 how we build relationships;

6 how we build shared success.

In most cases people make these decisions tacitly – without thinking and often driven by the curse of habit and conditioning. The road *to developing* our personal leadership means that we must step back and look again at how we deal with these six steps. Once we have *understood* this, we can then rethink what choices we would like to make and embark on a reconditioning process to enable us to make the optimum choices.

In work as in life, there's a progression. To be successful you need to be able to take others with you. This starts with learning to lead yourself. Once you have demonstrated that you're able to lead yourself effectively by the things you say and do, then you move into a position where you are leading others – possibly as a team leader. As you progress through the ranks in this guise you may find yourself stepping up to the next level, where you are asked to lead other leaders – to

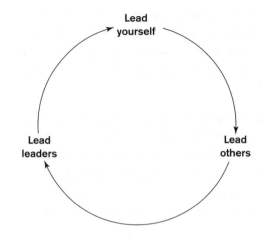

The leadership journey

step back and take a broader and often more challenging position.

What does it mean to lead yourself?

Personal leadership is often about mastery. To lead yourself effectively suggests that we have control over who we are and what we want to be – not to be the slave of others and ideally not to enslave ourselves without realizing it.

A degree of personal leadership or mastery does not happen by accident. It is a process that builds over time after serious thought and investment. Every day we come across opportunities to develop a greater degree of personal leadership: do I choose celery or chocolate; do I apologize after getting irritated and impatient; or do I choose to spend time with someone rather than being focused on the in-tray. These minor choices act as a small but significant investment in our ability to lead ourselves and from that lead others more effectively.

Every day we are given the gift of choice – and the free will to make the decision that either enhances or erodes our ability to become master of our own destiny. Each moment of our lives provides a chance to develop this mastery by setting a clear direction, looking at things and people in a new light and taking responsibility for who we are and what we want to be.

The risks of not taking ownership of choice is that we often abdicate the role of choice maker, because it is often so much easier to abscond and escape the pain of having to choose. Along with choice comes responsibility for the outcomes – it is often so much easier to let someone else own the decision, allowing us to blame them if something goes wrong.

People who own their choice can be said to internalize and operate from a self-concept that says, 'I take responsibility for both the good and the bad things that have happened in my life.' People who externalize take the view, 'I can't take responsibility for the good or bad outcomes because they stem from actions taken by other people.'

Most of us fall somewhere in the middle, believing that the life we have is a combination of our own effort and outside circumstances that affect the outcomes of events in our lives. So at times we are under the pressure of others and sometimes life is under our control.

For example, school students who have a very external idea of control often believe that it is solely the teacher's responsibility to teach them and not their responsibility to learn. Because they put the responsibility for learning on the teacher, they always fall under pressure of having to do rather than taking the choice to do things themselves.

Giving away choice

By abdicating choice and handing it over to others we are effectively giving our life to them. By virtue of giving them control over the choices we make we have enslaved ourselves. Although many people might not see it this way, many people quite readily slip into a form of slavery.

Back in the eighteenth century, people came from all over Britain to sign a contract with a master to serve a term of four to seven years overseas in the colonies. In exchange for this they received their passage paid from England, as well as food, clothing and shelter once they arrived. Some were even paid a salary. Once the contract was fulfilled they would be given their freedom along with small items to begin a new life. However, while in the indentured contract the person was considered his master's personal property and his contract could be inherited or sold. A master's permission was needed for everything from where they went and when, to how much money they kept.

Welcome to modern slavery

Let's now look at this in a modern light. So many people indenture themselves to an employer who has rights over who they are and what they do, restricts their freedom of the moment and controls their wage. Finally freedom is attained through retirement or redundancy, but by the time they are freed many people are institutionalized and find it difficult to find their feet as an independent human being.

This is not to suggest that working for someone else is an automatic state of slavery. Rather, in this sense, the slavery comes through the abdication of choice. The question is not about whether you work for someone, but whether you have the choice to leave! The problem comes when we get a job, and the first thing that happens is we take on debt, which offers luxury and a life that we have yearned for. But with the debt comes responsibility to repay the load, which in turn means we need the guarantee of a regular wage, which in turn means we cannot leave the job the next time we are bullied, harassed or are generally unhappy.

Even worse, along with the comfort of a decent wage and good job, we hand over choice for our development. The company will then invest in developing us to be great at what is important to them. But what happens when that need no longer exists? We are fully trained in the use of a product or process that has no value in the market. One of the biggest errors that I see people make on a daily basis is to hand over responsibility for their training to the employer. The real personal leader leads their life and ensures that they have all the necessary talent to survive and prosper irrespective of who they work for.

An alternative view is that being self-employed can have its own level of slavery, either to the bank, or to others who may be dependent on us. Taking the wrong decisions in a self-employment context can also lead to a form of slavery, witness the risky business programme where not much personal choice is being exhibited. Consider the small shopkeeper who opens their own business and relishes the freedom, only ten years later to curse the business because they can never have a decent holiday with their family because of the difficulty in finding staff they can trust. Indentured slavery is a deep and unseen force that can creep up on all of us, especially when we take our eye off the ball and forget to own our lives and development.

In essence, personal leadership is a tough route to follow. It is not an easier option and not one that can be plucked from the pages of the latest guru book. It is a daily investment that needs to be managed at a micro level. We are the choices we made yesterday and as a consequence we have to be focused on the choices we make every second of the day.

To help manage this choice the *Lead Yourself* framework highlights six factors that play a major role in this leadership journey. Importantly they are not the answer, but by thinking about them in more depth it might help ensure that the choices you make take you towards freedom and away from corporate slavery.

They are:

- **Choose your choice**. You might believe that you manage choice in your life, but the reality is that we often concede or trade away much of this power to others. Effective personal leadership is dependent on the extent to which we retain the ability to make choices.

- **Know where you are going.** There is little point in harnessing the power to make choices unless we know why we are making them. The aim is to define a set of clear personal goals and outcomes to use as criteria by which choices are made.

- **Map your map**. Don't just rely on your current map of the world. Constantly seek to discover and understand other people's maps so that you broaden your view and create more options and choices in the way you lead yourself and others.

- **Change how you change**. If you do what you always did, you will get what you always got. Your outcome might be clear, but the route to your end goal might offer challenges and barriers that you have never encountered before. For change to be effective and sustainable you need to learn how to manage it using alternative styles.

- **Step inside out**. To effectively deliver personal, sustainable success, you need to understand what success means for other people. To do this you have to step outside your view of the world and into theirs. Only when you understand how others think, feel and behave can you actually understand what success is like for them.

- **Share success**. Successful personal leadership is founded on the notion of shared outcomes and sustainable success. Personal leadership that is selfish or short-lived is not truly successful.

Be who you are

The ideas I try to introduce in this book are designed to help you *'be who you are and what you want to be'*.

For me this is the essence of personal leadership. To *'be who you are'* means to have a sense of personal purpose and to feel comfortable making choices that are right for you without the need to be a slave to other people's needs. It means that you have been able to shed the false doubts and assumptions that have been accumulated after many years of living and working with people who seek to lead through fear and force.

To *'be what you want to be'* means that you know where you are going, will love rather than tolerate change and are able to build great relationships with others so they are willing and able to help you on your journey. In this way you can effort-lessly get people to follow you not by coercion but through choice.

Once mastered, this enables you to lead others from a sense of confidence and authenticity rather than one of fear and force. As you help others to develop a sense of personal leadership you will automatically have taken a step onto the next level where you are a leader of leaders.

Whether a captain of industry, captain of a ship, or captain of the local football team, this ability to lead leaders is possibly one of the most enjoyable and beneficial outcomes of the journey to lead yourself.

01

choose your choice

Destiny is not a matter of chance, it is a matter of choice,
it is not a thing to be waited for, it is a thing to be
achieved.

William Jenning Bryan

OFTEN WE abstain from facing real decisions, instead leaving it to fate – effectively choosing not to choose.

What happens when you're driving along and someone pulls out in front of you? Do you get frustrated or angry? Most of the time we're able to contain these emotions but there are occasions when we let our emotions take over (each one of us can usually recall at least one occasion) and the red mist of anger leads us to take revenge on the perceived 'imbecile'. But the joy of retribution is often overtaken by the cold dawn of reality. It probably wasn't all their fault and, even if it was, the pain felt by the recipient of your outburst isn't going to help develop any future relationship.

Could we really have restrained our anger and controlled our feelings for that split second? Did we have a choice? It might be difficult, but difficult isn't the same as impossible. People can and do develop strategies to ensure that their emotions don't become harmful forces that take over their lives.

We also make non-choices in the way we think things through – very often when we're faced with a problem our standard solutions can't resolve. A prime example is children struggling with a homework problem. The schooling process often constrains students to process ideas and thoughts in a linear way. The moment they face a problem that is slightly outside their comfort zone they believe they don't know the answer and therefore can't solve it. Like someone stuck on an underground train that has broken down, they just sit and wait for someone else to come along and repair the fault and take them on their journey. Simply providing the answer offers only a short-term solution while creating a long-term predicament. It reinforces their belief that there is only one solution and that it is pointless to look for any other way to solve the issue, as well as reinforcing their intellectual dependency. By challenging them to think around the problem, they can be encouraged to learn to recognize that there are other choices and ways to resolve difficulties.

Finally, we can take non-choices in the way we behave. Think about the last time you got blinding drunk at the office party and woke up the next morning with the obligatory hangover and memory loss. You choose to blame the drink, the people who invited you, or the fact that it was the last Friday in the month and your pay-cheque had just arrived. The reality is that we choose to behave in such a way. At the point where the choice must be made (to have the Virgin Mary or Bloody Mary), we abstain from any sense of reality and choose not to take the better option.

In all of these examples, I have tried to look at instances where we may think, feel or behave in a way that seems 'normal'. However, normal isn't always good for us. We have the capacity to choose our choice, even when that choice seems uncomfortable, risky or confrontational. The test must always be: 'Am I making this choice based on what other people want, or am I responding in a way that fits what I really believe is correct?'

Within the 'choose your choice' decision there are three ideas to consider:

- **Push the pause button**. We have more power over the choices than we might believe – often it is about simply learning to push the pause button and put a temporary delay in what we are thinking, feeling or doing.

- **Choice muscle**. Choice is like a muscle, the more you use it the stronger it gets.

- **Choice pendulum**. Total choice gives you total freedom, but within such a position you can be seen as selfish. The essence is to balance your choice with the needs of others to reach a position where you share success.

- **The five choice faces**. So often we make choices that are driven by deep cognitive and emotional drivers and fail to realize quite the impact they have on the final decision.

Choose your choice is less about the freedom to choose actions, plans and journeys, and more about taking control of your inner thoughts and feelings. In the first instance, it's about giving yourself the power and freedom to choose your response to a given situation. You can choose how to respond to an irate customer, a crying child or an irritating relative who has just turned up on your doorstep. You can choose to behave in a negative way, but you have the capacity to choose your choices and respond in a more appropriate way. The acid test of a good choice is often: 'Will I look back in anger or regret at this decision?'

The Amish have the custom of ignoring or not responding to those who break their social code. They shun them and turn them into non-persons. Bear them in mind next time you receive poor service. You don't need to get upset or rant. You have the choice to simply say no, and choose not to go back to that place again. And don't imagine that avoiding confrontation has no consequence. The reality is that if they continue to offer the same poor service, the business will eventually fail. So, you don't need to get upset with people who upset you, you can just feel really good in the knowledge that you have erased them from your personal map. The message is don't shout – just shun.

Nor is developing the ability to make internal choices about how you feel, think and behave going to turn you into a sterile unfeeling robot. There's no need to spend hours carefully analyzing each problem. It will free your emotions up to think, feel or act in a away that will help you lead yourself and others in a far more effective way. Just choose not to bitch about your boss behind their back when they don't give you a good monthly review; choose not to get irate when there's a tricky problem to be solved; choose to say sorry to your boss or team member when you make a mistake.

Believe me, it's not just liberating, it's a lot less stressful.

Push the pause button

I used to work for someone who had a real problem. He would turn up every day at around 9.30 a.m., spend an hour in the office talking with his friends and then head off to the bar. When he got back around 2 p.m. he was well and truly over the driving limit. My problem was that if I couldn't get a morning slot in his diary I would end up with the afternoon slot. When this happened I would be frustrated because he was drunk and I wouldn't be able to get the message across to him. My response to my own frustration was either fight or flight. I would walk through the door ready to go into battle, or I would just send an email instead. Even when I got a morning slot, I was so uptight about the previous afternoon's session that I would always have a poor meeting. The red mist in front of my eyes ultimately led to me taking the first alternative job that I could find.

It dawned on me later that the failure was actually mine. I was being paid to deliver a product and clearly I let this person influence and reduce my capability to do this. I failed to choose my choice because I had failed to choose my response. I should have pushed the pause button and stopped to think about what I wanted to get out of the relationship; how I was reacting to his style; how I should be responding in order to achieve the goals I'd set for myself.

A key principle is that we have to choose our response to others' actions. I should have taken responsibility for my own behaviour – my own actions. On reflection I could have managed it in many different ways – but I let my responses be dictated by the other person's actions. As a result, my ability to operate effectively was reduced and I allowed someone else's behaviour to dictate my career path.

Consider times you look back and think 'if only' – 'if only I hadn't behaved that way or made that comment, it might be different now'. Just take an hour or so to look back at all the times you reacted or over-reacted to another person's emotions, ideas or behaviours. Try to think how else you might have behaved and what the consequences of that action might have been.

Clearly you can't choose the consequences of any actions you take, but you must be prepared to live with them, as they are a result of your behaviour. Not accepting the consequences means that you're trying to absolve yourself from both sides of the equation, and that's not possible.

Think about a relationship you have which is less than effective. Ask yourself: 'What do they do that I react to?' Try to think of a positive way in which you could react to their behaviour. Plan to put this reaction into practice the next time you meet them. If it doesn't work the first time, keep trying until it becomes a habit so you no longer respond to the things that trigger your irritation.

If we can develop the ability to push the pause button, then this is possibly the greatest single choice we can make. However, in doing this we have to learn how to pause three separate dimensions. Namely:

- how we feel (heart)
- how we think (head)
- how we behave (hand).

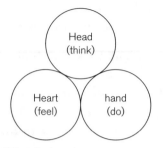

Figure 1.1 *Head, hand, heart*

Examples of the pause button being pushed in the three dimensions can be seen as:

The person who regularly suffers road rage symptoms will have to learn to push the pause button on their emotions (heart).

The junior manager who views the impending restructure as a signal that they will be made redundant will have to push the pause button on their thinking patterns (head).

The smoker who has given up for a week but still puts their hand out when cigarettes are offered will have to push the button on their habitual behaviour (hand).

It might be in this case that the parent seeks help because they believe they are not a good parent. The goal is to explore this belief and maybe focus more on the triggers. These can be extrinsic (baby crying, being alone, etc.) or intrinsic triggers (anxiety, stress, etc.). Once these triggers have been recognized and understood we can begin to introduce a 'pause point' to prevent the negative patterns that can be seen.

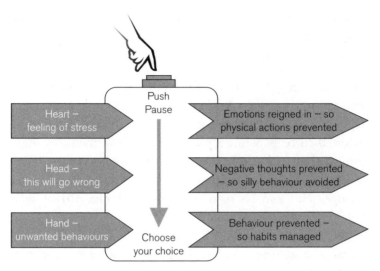

Figure 1.2 *Pause button*

Examples of other pause buttons might be helping the nervous presenter pause the stammering and fidgety hands by getting them to repeat a mantra over and over again; helping the nervous team member push a pause button when they first enter the office by developing a selection of casual conversation lines; or helping the person with low self-esteem by preparing a card that lists all their great attributes. The only right way to do this is the way that works for you. The trick is to understand yourself well enough to help prevent the spiral as it begins and understand where you can insert a pause and so stop the descent before you spiral out of control.

It is so often people's inability to choose their choice that causes many of the problems that they have to deal with. Dieting is often about choosing celery over chocolate;

promotion is about saying the right thing rather than getting angry with the boss; and gaining qualifications is about not being put off by the ice and snow.

The interesting thing is that the hardest part is to believe that you *can* push a pause button – if you believe that you can't then you won't try! Frequently people believe that some external force is acting upon them making them do these things. They will believe that when they are upset they 'have' to shout at someone, and that this is something they can never change. This can be seen with the road rage driver who believes that he has no control over the point between feeling angry with someone and hitting them. You need to understand that getting upset with someone doesn't mean you have to stop for an argument. If you can accept the principle that you do have choice, and that this choice extends to a micro level sitting between what you feel, think and do, then the hard part of the choose your choice process is complete.

The pause point

It is all very well to offer these ideas in the cold light of day, and say if you just do this then everything will be OK. However, I know only too well that there is a world of difference between knowing what to do to fix a problem and actually doing it. The dieter will know that they must not pick up the chocolate: the question is, will they know it before or after the event? Many (if not most) of you will be dealing with some form of addictive behaviour. This may not be full-on addiction in the sense of drugs, drink or debt, but addictive in the sense that you have developed really strong comfort patterns around a behaviour and so find it difficult to let go.

The trick is to step back from the pause point and try to view it from a wider temporal plane. When people are in the pit of confusion, self-doubt and despair all they tend to see is what is happening now, forgetting everything else that has taken place. Talk with the person who has just been made redundant, the middle-aged man whose partner has just walked out or the teenager who has failed their driving test for the third time. All they will see is a huge flashing beacon in front of their eyes saying 'YOU HAVE FAILED AND WILL ALWAYS FAIL'. This beacon is so bright that it is all they can see.

In managing the pause point it is key to step back from this beacon, turn down the intensity and instead take a broader look at what has happened. You can do this by using the 5-point pause model. Take any topic where someone habitually does something that they later regret. This might be someone dealing with road rage, poor presentations or a nervous interviewee. In all these cases there is a common cycle as shown in Figure 1.3.

If we take the road rage driver, they might be driving down the road without a care in the world and happily listening to the radio (Point 1 – pre stage). As they approach some roadworks a long queue has built up so they crawl slowly along with everyone else. However, they have been in situations before where people tend to come down alongside the queue and try to cut in at the very end. They remember this and begin to get wound up at the thought of it and start to

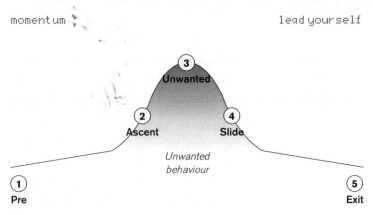

Figure 1.3   *Pause point model*

look in the side mirror for anyone who might try to do this. This begins to raise their emotional anxiety (heart) and the negative thoughts (head) kick in as they are expecting the worst to happen. At this point they have shifted to Point 2 on the model (ascent). Finally, it happens. Along comes the driver who tries to cut in the front. Because our driver is already well up the ascent stage, all it takes is an arrogant look from the other driver and they are at Point 3 – with the unwanted feelings, thoughts and behaviours kicking in. They are out of the car screaming and shouting at the other driver. Luckily the driver manages to speed off and the first driver gets back into the car and begins the slide down the other side of the hump. At Point 4 they might experience a mixture of thoughts and feelings. There might be satisfaction because they 'gave them what for' or they might want to return to Point 3 and give chase, to sort it out for good. Finally they drive off and begin to calm down and revert to the pre-hump stage. Now at Point 5 (exit) they might begin to regret what had happened and curse themselves for falling into the trap of road anger – something they have been trying to deal with for years.

The trick is to not give up and just decide that the problems cannot be resolved. Instead, they should reflect on what happened and chart the change they experience over a time frame. Once charted they can agree at what point they actually pushed the pause button. They might have pushed it at Point 5. Although too late to stop the action taking place, the great thing is that they pushed it. They can then decide at what point they would like to push it next time. If someone has deeply embedded habits, it might well be sufficient to aim for a Point 4 pause next time. Hence the choice might not be about stopping the behaviour, rather it is about helping to manage the pause points. Eventually they should get to the stage where they are able to push the pause button on the ascent stage and then ideally at the pre stage – the moment they feel themselves beginning to climb the hump.

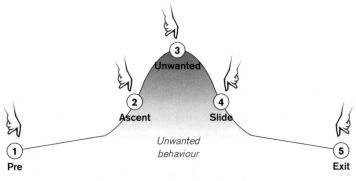

Move pause point back along the timeline

Figure 1.4 *Managed pauses*

By understanding the five key stages in the pause model, the person can be aware of reversion and understand when the bad habits are creeping in and what they can do about it. No matter what choice you want to make, where someone is trying to change a bad habit into a good one then the pause pattern will probably be visible. The presenter who makes a mess and then recognizes the error just as it went wrong or the manager who has reprimanded someone when it wasn't really their fault. The more the person is able to learn the pause process the greater chance they have of managing themselves when faced with addictive forces. Even if the client hits the pause button in the slide stage and after the negative action has been taken, it doesn't matter, because that is better than hitting the pause button at the exit stage. By learning to hit at the slide stage they will be able to learn to hit the pause button at the unwanted stage, and with practice will be able to do this with some ease. The pause framework is to help the person appreciate that they do have the choice to choose their responses and that it is never too late to choose.

Choice muscle

As you start to flex your ability to make choices, a powerful transformation will occur. Just like the growing strength of a muscle, the ability to make small choices leads to an enhanced capacity for bigger and bigger choices. So, as you enhance your desire and ability to lead yourself, this in turn enhances your ability to lead others. People will sense that you have a level of strength and discipline in your life and will look to you for support and guidance.

Just think about the people you turn to for advice and assistance. You probably picked them because you recognized intuitively that they have the ability to make choices when facing difficult circumstances. The more you choose to choose, the more, in turn, you'll be asked to help with the choices others have to make. The possibilities are endless. You'll make contact with more and more people who have the capacity to choose their choice and you'll help people transform their lives. The world you'll be operating in will be characterized by freedom, challenge and alternatives.

We can choose to choose

The only choice they give you is one you gave them in the first place. So don't be thankful when your company says it's going to allow you more space to make decisions or that they are going to run an empowerment programme. This is a capability you already have, and your taking up their 'offer' is just an indication of how much personal choice and control you have traded away.

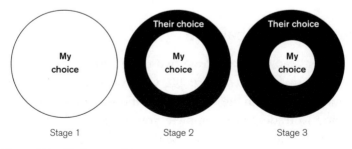

Figure 1.5 *Choice muscle*

Choice is lost over time though gradual erosion (see Figure 1.5). In childhood, we have the absolute beliefs that we have the freedom to make decisions we believe are right. As a child we want what we want, and we want it now and we'll scream the supermarket down if we don't get it. Erosion starts when we have to adhere to the constraints and disciplines of other people, for example, parents and teachers looking for the most painless ways to manage their lives. As we start school and work we have to trade in our right to choose in order to ensure some level of success. Then, at some point, the choices we have traded away exceed the freedoms we are left with. The net result is that we are in the choice trap. We have given away our freedom to make choices and the only way to recover it is to give up the trappings of success we had so eagerly pursued.

The way to stretch our choice muscle is to draw a personal leadership boundary. Part of this decision will involve a risk and reward trade-off. But you can't have your cake and eat it.

If your company has paid to take over your right of choice in certain areas, you must return something in order to regain control of those aspects that are important to you.

A question of balance

The first step is easy – draw two circles. In the inner circle, write those aspects of your life where you want to choose your choice, and in the outer one put those aspects that you're happy to trade. Once complete you should end up with a picture like the one in Figure 1.6.

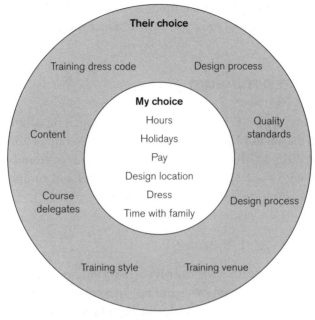

Figure 1.6 *Choice wheel*

The idea is for you to take back the things that choice erosion has taken over during your lifetime. Don't worry, you don't have to give your car to charity to rid yourself of material slavery. But before you can start to lead yourself, you do have to recognize the extent to which you have given away your freedom of choice. If you're happy in a situation where the outer circle overlaps with your inner circle because it offers you the financial freedom and comfort you desire, then fine. But you'll need to understand the balance between the two and the risks that go with your level of choice. You have the right to choose the boundaries of your choice area; the important thing is to take time to understand just what the boundaries are and how you can influence them.

Choice pendulum

Think of choice as a pendulum – any degree of misalignment puts the swing out of kilter and the clock out of time. A pendulum retains its stability because it moves from left to right with a swing that is constant in travel and timing and centres around a balanced centre point.

Balance and alignment

When we abstain, consciously or subconsciously, or trade options on our lives, we can end up corporate slaves. The pendulum is pulled over to the far right-hand side (see Figure 1.7). In this position, you have little real choice in your life and it's difficult to pull back to a position of control.

If you allow the pendulum to swing in the other direction, it's just as unstable and likely to topple over (see Figure 1.8). The danger is that the choose-your-choice message can be taken too literally. Imagine the person who's totally wrapped up in their ability to control and manage every single aspect of their life. They might be a real kingpin in terms of life management but you'd avoid them like the plague. An over-zealous approach to the choose-your-choice dimension can result in your being seen as selfish and egotistical.

A sense of balance needs to be achieved by taking a mid-way position. You take a stance based on a collaborative and inter-

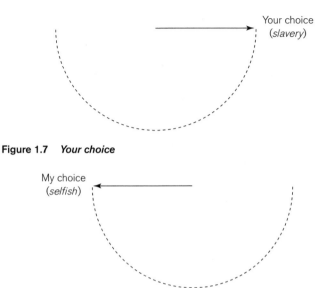

Figure 1.7 *Your choice*

Figure 1.8 *My choice*

active approach that allows you to make your personal choices in the spirit of sharing. As a spouse or partner, parent, manager or coach, for example, you make your own choices where the others in the relationship are concerned, but when formulating your decision, it's made on the basis of a shared set of values and principles.

All long-term effective relationships are grounded in the position where all the parties have attained the power to choose their choice. By shifting to a shared-choice position the individuals are not giving up any power within their personal leadership. Much of the driving force for a balanced, centred position stems from the in-security (inner security) driver. If someone is driven by their personal insecurity, they will be

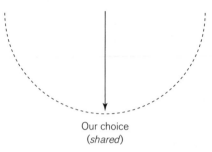

Our choice
(*shared*)

Figure 1.9   *Our choice*

loath to share choice because it feels as though they are losing power over their lives. Where the in-security driver drives someone, they are happy to share choice and power because they are comfortable that all their personal power comes from within.

When both parties lose the power to choose their choice and in effect give control to the other person, it places the relationship in a weak position. It leads to a spirit of second-guessing, double-checking, unspoken arguments and undis-cussable feelings. If you see evidence of this type of behaviour in any relationship, look for signs of choice imbalance. Someone is not managing their right and freedom to make choices.

Think about the people you work or live with. Imagine where you would place each of them on the choice pendulum. Do they operate from a selfish basis and make decisions based on their needs only? Do they always watch their choice of TV channel? Buy the food they like? Or do they always make decisions influenced by what you want? Maybe there's someone who works for you and all they ever do is agree with you? Perhaps you choose to work or live with these people because you're locked into a relationship or because they satisfy a particular need in you. But the question to ask yourself is: to what extent are you really taking control of the situation and leading yourself and them? Would the relationship be even more effective if you were able to share choices? Could you agree what things are important for you and for the others in the relationship and then make more choices based on this shared understanding?

You can hit the target

We have a choice in how we allocate our emotions and energy. Next time you're in a meeting and people start to lament the failure of the senior managers or 'them up there', choose not to go there, focus on the real issues instead. Challenge the group to map what is in their power to resolve, and what factors are beyond their control. Then work on what you can do.

The beauty is that as the group becomes more practised at operating in the 'can' and 'convince' areas (see Figure 1.10) it will automatically self-correct and fix itself when the vague 'can't' issues surface. The net result is that the emotions of the group will be energized, there will be improved decision-making capability, and deliverable actions will be agreed, not pie-in-the-sky solutions. As a group you'll make the decision to choose your choice.

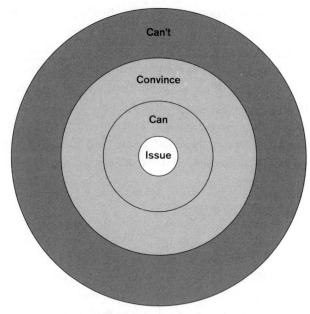

Figure 1.10 *Can't convince*

Colourblind choices

Hardly anybody really makes a choice in the way that textbooks suggest we should. In my entire professional career, time as a musician and head of training and consulting firm I have almost never seen 'proper' decision making taking place. It is nearly always a ramshackle mix and match of various models and practices. I know only too well just how hard it is to understand the process of making a choice; and that the whole concept of 'rational decision making' never really seems to hit the spot in terms of describing how things really are. Even when, in one of my other books, I offer what

I believe to be a robust decision-making model for consul-
tancy solutions, I know just how hard it is to take a theoretical
model and apply it within the human soup of decision
making. We know that it is best to define the choice criteria,
generate options, rank the option and then select a solution.
The process is highly logical, intellectual and visible but so
rarely progresses smoothly.

The reality is that emotion and reason tend to work together
at differing levels to impact in the way the choice is being
made and the selection of the final outcome. We know that
anger, fear and excitement all conspire to influence any
choice-making process. Sometimes it is important to listen to
the emotions and take what they say into account – at other
times we have to let go of them and be driven by a logical
choice. The point is that when people make choices – be they
managing directors, doctors or parents – they are acting as
human beings, driven by the same forces that have acted
upon us since we emerged from the swamps.

Think about the various television reality programmes where
people have a dream to 'get a place in the sun' only to realize
after a few months that maybe they have made a mistake and
the truth dawns that the choice was flawed. Think about the
various choices that you have made in your life, this month or
even today. Just why it is that one moment the decision
seemed so perfect and unflawed – but one minute, hour or
day later you look back in amazement and just can't understand why it made so much sense at the time. This is often
because we are all driven by deep drivers that impact on the
way we make choices. Although there are many drivers,
two that can have a significant impact are the emotional/

cognitive dimensions and the optimistic and pessimistic drivers. The suggestion here is that at any point when we are making a decision any one of four forces will be acting upon the choice-making process – often without our realizing it. The four forces are: affective driver (heart); cognitive driver (head); optimistic driver and pessimistic driver.

Affective driver (heart)

A common view of the nature of emotions and in particular the school of thought around emotional intelligence is based on the premise that a part of the human brain called the *amygdala* does a great deal of work when managing human emotions. These responses mostly occur automatically, as in the case of the familiar fight-or-flight response triggered by threatening situations. Humans have evolved in such a way that a 'neural-hijacking' takes place that provides a quick answer to life's critical situations. As such the *amygdala* has links with the neocortex, which can accordingly exert some control over the largely automatic responses of the brain. The amount of control has a genetic component; yet one can learn to control emotions to a certain degree. Most people do learn this at some point. Further, it is possible to hone the skill, achieving greater abilities to manage emotions.

As you read this page, pause for a second and reflect on what you are feeling. Are you relaxed and almost serene because you have taken the day off and ignored all the washing-up and jobs to be done around the house; are you slightly anxious because the train is late and you are worried that you might be late to the office for the third day running; are you buzzing because the envelope arrived this morning which announced the result for the exams you recently took; or are you somewhat wistful or low because it is the anniversary of a time when something sad happened in your life? You may not be overtly conscious of these feelings, but they are there and their presence will clearly impact on how you read this book and any choices you make in the next five minutes.

From a leadership perspective it is important to understand our emotions and how they act as factors that drives what we do. We have all been in the situation of thinking rationally through what we will say or do when faced with a particular situation, only to find that when push comes to shove, the fight/flight mechanism will kick in and our response actually has little to do with the planned behaviour. It is at this point that the emotional rudder has taken hold and directed what we are thinking and doing. Typical emotions that we face on a daily basis include:

Anxiety	Fear	Love
Anger	Guilt	Pride
Disgust	Happiness	Rage
Depression	Hope	Surprise
Excitement	Hate	

When thinking about choosing we need to be aware of our emotional state and the impact it will have on the choices we make.

Cognitive driver (head) –

As you read this page, stop and think about what you are thinking. What is that little inner voice saying about you, the book and your interpretation of the content? Are you agreeing with the ideas and thinking about how to apply it; do you have negative views because you have heard the ideas before and can't see anything new in the book; or do you think that the ideas are too complex and that leadership is an instinctive thing that doesn't really benefit from the use of models and theories? You may not be overtly conscious of these thoughts, but they exist and their presence will clearly affect how you read this book, the choices you form and any consequent actions you take.

People generally do not understand the effects of their own thoughts. Hence it is crucial to expose what impact the thought patterns have on our behaviour. To help do this we can learn to understand the cognitive structures that underpin how people make sense of the world.

A key principle in the leadership framework is that external events do not cause people to be act or feel in a certain way. The spider cannot make me scared and the sight of blood cannot make me feel ill – this is my chosen response to the extrinsic trigger. So it is people's interpretation of the external trigger that causes them to act in a certain way. Imagine how two people can see the same film, eat the same meal or date the same person but their chosen responses and perceived experiences will be fundamentally different.

We often form this interpretation automatically, without any conscious effort. Like the autopilot on a plane, the pilot and crew can sit back and operate on the assumption that a computer is taking all the most appropriate choices for them. In the same way we all have an autopilot mode – where we let pre-programmed responses to external triggers kick into place without consciously challenging what is happening. However, in the same way that the professional pilot will always keep a watchful eye on the autopilot to ensure it is not taking erroneous decisions, we all need to keep a watchful eye on the thought patterns used to take what appear to be simple choices and actions. These can be seen in the constant flow of thoughts, ideas, beliefs and dialogue that take place in the background while we are managing life. As an example, while reading this book you have been saying things to yourself; points you agree with, disagree with, thoughts about things you can and can't do in relation to the sugges-tions in the book. That is your autopilot – the guiding voices that drive how you feel and behave.

As leaders we need to understand, interpret and in some cases modify these thoughts. This is because some will be positive and help us achieve our desired outcome. But some will be counterproductive and act as a barrier to achieving the outcome. Importantly these thoughts are not bad thoughts as such, they are natural cognitive processes that we all have, and the challenge is to help understand those that aid their journey and those that inhibit it. They can look like:

- *That girl is really good looking – she won't speak to me*
- *I don't think the manager will give me a good review*
- *I can't do this*
- *Life is good – so maybe I will book another holiday*

- *The board really like my ideas – that will lead to another promotion.*

As leaders of ourselves and others we must learn how to map our thoughts and, once mapped, to differentiate between those autopilot routines that are helping and those that are disabling the journey.

Very often people are not aware of their entrenched head maps – they just exist and are used as a guide to drive our choice making processes. These beliefs might be things like *'always win'* or *'life sucks'*. These deep and rigid beliefs can cause us to feel stressed because our views leave no room for variety in how we see the world. To improve how we make choices it is important to recognize and accept that any rigid views that exist start to challenge and change those that are limiting our ability to progress.

Internal negotiation

Hence, everything we say and do (hand) is driven by a combination of our cognitive (head) and affective (heart) dimensions. Although everybody has head and heart dimensions that drive their behaviour, some pay more attention to their thoughts than to their feelings, while others pay more attention to their feelings than to their thoughts.

In Homer's *The Odyssey*, Ulysses is faced with a classic interpersonal conflict. He knows he will soon encounter the Sirens – the mythical female enchantresses who try to lure seafaring men to their island and to the eventual death. These nymphs had the power of charming by their song all who heard them, so that mariners were impelled to cast themselves into the sea to destruction. Circe directed Ulysses to stop the ears of his seamen with wax, so that they should not hear the strain; to have himself bound to the mast, and to enjoin his people, whatever he might say or do, by no means to release him till they should have passed the Sirens' island. Ulysses obeyed these directions. As they approached the Sirens' island, the sea was calm, and over the waters came notes of music so ravishing and attractive that Ulysses struggled to get loose and, by cries and signs to his people, begged to be released; but they, obedient to his previous orders, sprang forward and bound him still faster. They held on their course, and the music grew fainter until it could no longer be heard, at which point Ulysses joyfully gave his companions the signal to unseal their ears, and they released him from his bonds.

With this Ulysses manages his competing preferences. He knows that his heart will pull him to listen to the music but his head says not to listen, else he will die. This internal contradiction or inconsistency is one he faced and was able to resolve. Unfortunately, it is a negotiation that so many people fail to resolve. The alcoholic wants a drink and knows they should not; Eve wanted the apple but knew she should not eat it; I don't want to get up in the morning but know I have to in

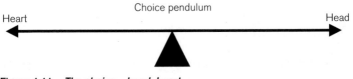

Choice pendulum

Heart   Head

Figure 1.11 *The choice – head, heart*

order to make a living. These two dimensions can be seen as impulse (heart) and reason (head).

As such, every second of the day people are choosing between what they want to do and what they should do as seen in the choice pendulum above. Think of when we go shopping, which is often a constant turmoil of want and should. I want the king prawns, but should get the cheap prawns to save money; want the expensive cut of meat, but should get the cheap cut so that it will go further. Often these 'want' and 'should' drivers are driven by short- and long-term payback or discounting factors. People may want to act in a way that satisfies immediate needs but feel they should look for the long-term payback in order to be sensible.

As we begin to understand the nature of these differing drivers we can see how a preference for a logical or emotional perspective will drive a preferred choice.

The challenge you face as a leader is to understand that inside you may be two people: the logical rational person who would use language such as 'what should you do' or 'what is best to manage'; and the emotional person who needs you to ask 'How do you feel?' and 'What do you want?' In addition to this, you must be aware of the dual personality inside others and how their own head and heart preferences will drive the choices they make.

Optimistic driver

The optimistic driver is quite simply that – it is when we view the world as an oyster and see everything from a positive perspective. This might be the rose-tinted glasses optimism when we simply put a more positive spin on the message we give or hear. Or it might be the full-on 'everything is perfect' viewpoint where nothing can go wrong. Ambrose Bierce defined optimism from this perspective as the doctrine or belief that everything is beautiful, including what is ugly.

Pessimistic driver

Running counter to this is the pessimistic driver, or the view that everything that can go wrong will. This driver can have a quite debilitating impact on the choice process as highlighted by Helen Keller when she suggested that no pessimist ever discovered the secret of the stars or sailed an uncharted land, or opened a new doorway for the human spirit. The problem is that this driver can have the ability to creep up on people and to catch them unawares: the person who has been unemployed for a few weeks and fears they will never work again or the singer who drops a note in the concert and walks off stage because they fear that people will have no faith in their ability.

Maybe a nice and simple way to wrap up these two drivers is to pick on the point made by Sir Winston Churchill when he suggests that a pessimist sees the difficulty in every opportunity; an optimist sees the opportunity in every difficulty. The challenge from a choice perspective is which driver is having most impact at any given moment, how do you know, is it the optimum driver or do you need to shift the perspective.

The four choices

In considering the four drivers of heart, head, optimistic and pessimistic we can use this to create a choice model that helps understand why we make certain choices at certain moments in time. At any moment in time the four forces shown in the figure will be driving a particular choice.

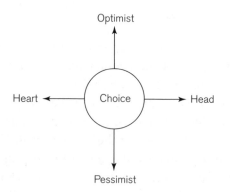

Figure 1.12 *Pessimist, optimist*

The effective leader will be able to determine how the four forces are acting upon them at any time and take steps to move their affective and cognitive states to the optimum position, but to do this they need to understand the first point which is to determine which forces are most dominant. We can help this by building a simple representative model of the point at which the four forces meet.

When we consider the four quadrants that emerge from the conjunction of the four forces we get the following quadrants:

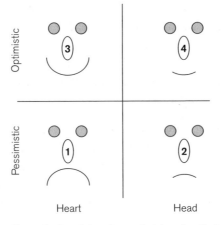

Figure 1.13   *Faces for head, heart, pessimist and optimist*

1 **Pessimistic Heart**. A choice that is characterized by a negative emotional view of a situation. This might be the sense of doom that the teenager feels after getting a poor exam result. They can't characterize exactly what it is they feel – but it is a sense of waste and futility.

2 **Pessimistic Head**. This can be seen in the negative thought patterns that may go through the golfer's head as they approach the hole that always causes them a problem. This might be inner voices saying that it will go wrong again or maybe time to give up and go to the bar.

3 **Optimistic Heart**. Here someone has simply woken up feeling great – the sun is shining, no bills on the hall carpet and the lottery turned up trumps with a small win. It is hard to say exactly how the emotional optimism manifests itself – it is just there and can have a profound effect on the choices made.

4   **Optimistic Head**. This can be seen in the positive mental
    models that can float through people's heads and affect
    their behaviour in a significant way. So the sales agent who
    has just made their third sale is driven by the thought
    patterns that they are on a roll and the next three sales will
    also go their way as well.

The importance of these four quadrants cannot be under-
stated in understanding the choice process. Imagine someone
faced with a major choice in their life – like a team member
who has to make a choice about the forthcoming managerial
vacancy, i.e. whether or not to apply for the vacancy.

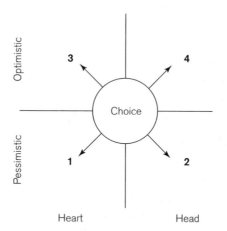

Figure 1.14   *Choice pendulum, heart, head, pessimist, optimist*

1   If they slip into quadrant 1 then the choice may be driven
    by fear of the responsibilities and worry about the diffi-
    culties that would face them. The net result is that they
    send a panic email to their boss saying that they are really
    not interested in getting promotion.

2 If the choice is driven by quadrant 2 then they may not have any fear, but after thinking about the promotion they might start to reflect on the difficult issues, question their perceived lack of qualifications or listen to gossip from other people who cast doubt on the longevity of the job. Again, the member drops a more considered note to their manager explaining why they don't believe that this post is suitable for them.

3 When driven by quadrant 3 they take one look at the advert, and because their day has gone so well, immediately decide to go for the job and are so buoyed by their inner confidence that they start to talk about their chances of getting the job and heavily infer that they are full of confidence about getting the job. The danger with this is that they can start to appear cocky and face a potential backlash in the interview.

4 Finally, if they are driven by quadrant 4, after thinking about the job they conclude that based on their skills and experience it should be theirs for the taking. They send an email to their boss and their boss's boss indicating their desire to apply and also offering the reasons why they believe they will be the best person for the job.

With all of these choices, it is not a case of any being better or worse than the others, it is more a case of understanding the impact that the various dimensions have on their choice and, importantly, whether they will look back with regret at a later date.

Quadrant 5 choice

The suggestion is that one way to not look back in anger or regret is to draw upon the advice offered by Albert Schweitzer. He suggests that an optimist is a person who sees a green light everywhere, while a pessimist sees only the red stoplight. The truly wise person is colourblind. The essence with this being that you choose to ignore the positive and negative forces and also balance out the heart and head drivers.

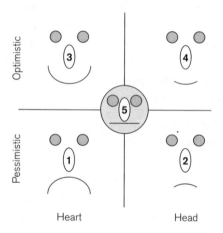

Figure 1.15 *The fifth quadrant*

By choosing to sit in quadrant 5, i.e. in the centre position of the model then you are offered a number of benefits:

1   There is a balance in your decision making and you are not clouded by the strength of the four forces.

2 You have the option to make short forays into the various quadrants – just to offer an alternative perspective on the choice. There can be a huge benefit in deliberately stepping into each quadrant in order to gain a range of broader perspective on your choice.

3 You are more able to discern what quadrants are driving other people's choices. For example you hear that redundancy is looming and run to quadrant 1 – *your colleague also runs* to quadrant 1 – the odds are that you will formulate plans that seem sensible but are actually biased by a negative emotional response.

Although this whole process can sound very simple, in many cases it is quite the opposite. Taking the standard phrase that the fish are the last to see the water (because they swim in it), you will often be the last person to see the mood you are in. It can take a great deal of courage to be prepared and able to step outside yourself and look back to really understand what forces are acting upon how you are making a choice. However, the upside is that you really do begin to gain control and choose how you choose. No longer can choices be seen as a product of your DNA or environment – they are deliberate and positive actions that develop a greater sense of personal leadership and also help others to lead themselves more effectively.

Choose your choice – the three levels

Leader of leaders	**Lead leaders** – Help make choice a valued process and not one buried deep in management processes.
Leader of others	**Lead others** – Help others to take responsibility for their choices and outcomes. Be careful you don't create slaves by letting them abdicate choice.
Leader of self	**Lead yourself** – Realize that you always have choice – the trick is to understand how best to use it.

Choose your choice: quick summary

The key aspects to consider in this area include:

1   Other people can't give you freedom of choice. You start life with a full box of choices and as you grow older you may choose to barter them away in exchange for other benefits. Other people only exercise control over your choices because you allow them to.

2   The life you have today is a product of the choices you have made. The life you want tomorrow will be achieved with the choices you make today. Choose your next choice carefully.

3   By choosing your choice you increase your personal power. Ultimately you will influence the people who have influence over you.

4 You own and are responsible for the impact of your choices and their consequences.

5 Sometimes choice is about not taking action or responding to the way that others behave towards you. It's harder to say 'I won't' than it is to say 'I will'.

6 Choice isn't always about what you want to do; you can choose to create a shared success with other partners.

7 Your most important choices involve disregarding the things you can't change and concentrating on the things you can.

choice two

know where you are going

There are two kinds of people,
those who finish what they start, and so on.

Robert Byrne

WE ALL have a guiding force that helps make life choices. In his book *Working with Emotional Intelligence*, Daniel Goleman talks about the inner rudder, the ability to make intuitive decisions based on subjective hunches or gut feelings. This rudder guides who we are, where we are heading and what course we can take.

This rudder is a powerful thing because small changes in its direction effect awesome control over the craft. When it malfunctions, the consequences can be pretty disastrous. At height, it's possible for the pilot to correct errors and take back control of the plane, but lower down the consequences can be disastrous because the pilot doesn't have time to take remedial action.

Sometimes you can lose control of your inner rudder and suffer similar consequences. At best, the rudder might be slightly off-centre, producing circular patterns in your life which means you end up going round in circles, never quite achieving what you set out to do. Decisions are made and seem to make sense in isolation but, because they lack a guiding sense or vision, you end up going back over previous journeys and never quite realizing your potential. You might believe you have control, but in reality any decision is being made by the bow-wave effect of the previous decision.

In a worst-case scenario, your inner rudder is unshackled and flops from side to side. The result is that you're buffeted by external forces, losing the ability to make clear decisions. So you go through life constantly trying to get hold of new opportunities but always failing to make any real headway.

Like many people, I spent my early life being guided by the wishes of my parents. I even went into the same company as my father. Later, I succumbed to the drives of society, had a family and had a struggle to make ends meet. Only after I turned 38 did I really start to question what my driving goal had been, what it was then, and most importantly, what it should be for the rest of my life.

I had to grab hold of the rudder while the boat was flailing around in a force-eight gale with water leaking over the sides. But when you finally gain control, it's a real pleasure.

Who controls your rudder?

Have you ever considered who really controls your rudder, to what extent you have control and in what way you've ceded control to others? Have they wrested it from your grasp, or have you given it up voluntarily? Consider the following questions:

- Who chooses when you go on holiday?
- Who chooses how you dress in the morning?
- Who chooses where and when you work?
- Who chooses how much you earn?
- Who chooses your next job?

- Who chooses your career direction?

- Who chooses who you are?

Can you really claim to have absolute control over all of these areas? If the answer is 'Yes', then you do have a clear sense of choice and direction in your life. If, however, there are areas where you're not so sure, maybe you've given or traded away parts of your life to others. You probably made the exchange in return for a benefit, possibly a comfortable work life, high wages or a stake in the company. But, now you've traded partial control of your inner rudder to someone else, how happy are you? Is it a shared journey or do they tend to make all the key decisions? And can you regain control?

My concern is that as we go through life trading off parts of our inner rudder, we start to lose a sense of who we are. The net result is that rather than enhancing our personal security, we are potentially increasing our sense of insecurity, and consequently our vulnerability.

Rudder ownership: from insecurity to in-security

In many ways the direction we choose is driven by the confidence we have in ourselves to achieve our end goal. This is often about the level of comfort or security we have in who we are and what we do. So, where do you get your feel-good factor and what happens when it disappears? Do you (or would you) perceive yourself to be a success in life because you earn a certain amount, have a BMW or live in a certain area? If so, what happens when that is taken away from you?

Think about the people who marry film stars. Are they marrying that person for who they are or what they do? What happens when their fame fades?

The problem is that we measure each other and ourselves by what we have and do, rather than who we are. Think about the last time you went to a party and met someone new. The odds are that early on in the conversation one of your questions was 'What do you do for a living?' or 'Where do you work?' This desire to label people and put them in a category based on what they do or how they earn a living is endemic in society and unfortunately conditioned from quite an early age. It is not uncommon in school for children to compare their dads' wages, and unofficial playground status is allotted accordingly.

Look around and all you will see is role confusion, as people fall into the trap of confusing who they are with what they do, and we rely on these false badges of office. Look out for people on discussion or news programmes. As someone is being interviewed their name and job title flash up on the screen. From this limited piece of information we are left to infer who this person is, their relevance to the discussion, their value to society and to themselves, and a whole host of other social badges that confer various degrees of status. For those lucky enough to have an impressive title, we can infer not only that they know what they're talking about, but also that they know more than we do. Only when we get up close and take a personal view do we start to challenge this ficti-tious belief and remember that the title is only a symbol of what they deliver in one unique situation. It's not an indication of who they really are.

Black holes of insecurity

The pull of these external security blankets that society provides is like the gravitational pull of a black hole. They have enormous energy, and the closer you get, the stronger the gravitational pull becomes, to a point where it's impossible to break away.

Try drawing a map of your life and consider the different black holes of insecurity you're attracted to (see Figure 2.1). These are the goals, needs and desires that demand your time, energy and money – you believe you've 'made it' once you

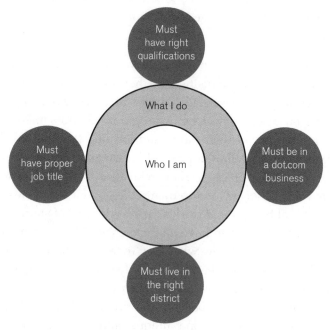

Figure 2.1 *Who am I?*

have them. Their upside is the personal satisfaction and buzz you get from having them; the downside is that, as with an addiction, you always have to have more.

I've seen it so many times with people who believe their goal in life is to get promoted. When you ask them why, they don't really know. It's just the gravitational pull from the you-must-have-a-powerful-job-title black hole that drives the need for importance. This drive for a corporate badge was highlighted in a survey of 1,500 workers where 70 per cent said they would rather have a fancier job title than a pay rise. It's increasingly absurd, isn't it? If your company doesn't have a Paperclips Tzar, it probably has a Vice-President of Photo-copying . . .

In many ways, grand titles could bring more fun and creativity into organizations – like the Raging Inexorable Thunder Lizard Evangelist for a vice-president at the University of Texas Medical School – but few companies encourage this kind of creativity and, instead, titles are used as a substitute for the personal strength that comes from knowing who you are. The real danger is when people believe that the power assigned to the title has been mystically trans-muted to them and that they carry this power wherever they go.

In one organization I know, people were assigned operational codes that indicated their status. Each code consisted of up to three letters and three numbers in sequence. The make-up of the code meant that by simply looking to see how many characters were in the code, you could immediately determine the level of the individual within the corporate hierarchy. So if your designation was 'B', that would put you at director level, whereas AB1 might put you as a relatively senior manager, and ABC123 meant that you were the lowest of the low, generally a line manager. In meetings, people would introduce themselves, and they would immediately reel off their name and corporate code. To the uninitiated this might be seen as a minor issue, but it was a powerful tool for people to set the pecking order in a meeting. The coup de grâce would be the really senior manager who would hold back on his code until everyone else had said theirs before announcing his own with a grand flourish, like a wise old wizard pronouncing his status through the size of his wand.

In-security

Once you understand the principles contained in this book, no longer will the idea of insecurity be a negative and worrying concept. Instead, in-security, or inner-security, will mean what it says – that your personal security comes from within.

We need a form of leadership that draws on our ability to discard any notion of dependence on other people and objects. We've spent too much of our working lives scared – scared that we'll be laid off, yelled at or blamed for something that wasn't our fault. And what have we learned? Fear doesn't motivate us for long. In his book *Free-Agent Declaration of Independence*, Daniel H. Pink suggests that performers become great by playing in their own terror-free zone. We all have terror zones where demons reign, but we have the choice to face them head-on, recognize them for what they are, and then exorcize them. The first step to shift from insecurity to in-security is to choose your choice.

Personal leadership is founded in the notion that we should have a clear and defined outcome for any journey, that is, know where we're going. This clarity will offer a clear and purposeful vision to ourselves and others. I am not suggesting that everything we do in life should be rigidly controlled with a finite and planned outcome, just that we should aspire to know what we want to achieve and why. In developing a clear goal for our personal or business life we can take away the pain of indecision, overcome insecurity, and avoid the confusion that arises when we are pulled in different directions. Although you might believe that you know where you're going, there is often a deeper internal tension that pulls you in many directions.

Think about the last time you had to make an important decision. Did you feel any unease about making the choice? If you did, then the different parts of you were trying to make the decision in competition with each other.

We lead three lives, each driven by the three dimensions of heart, head and hand. The hand is the part of us that others see. The head view is how we think, the rational. The heart is how we feel, or the third, secret inner life that only we know. When aligned, we have a clear sense of purpose. We can make a decision almost without thinking because the dimensions are working together. But when the heart, head and hand journeys are separated it leads to internal tension and frustration, and in turn anxiety or guilt.

Imagine you've just won the lottery. How will you spend the money? The heart says take those flying lessons you've dreamed of since you were a child. The head suggests stocks and shares. The hand choice might be to do what your friends suggest and have a party, just blow it all on the biggest gig in town. This indecision and dilemma might last for a second or it might last for a year. However long, such internal debate can lead to anxiety and tension both internally and in all your relationships. (PS: Opt for the party!)

Where you have clear personal purpose, such indecision will be minimized. You'll know where you're going, have a clear outcome and be able to describe to others what's important now and in the future. Once you have such a clear and unambiguous view of your journey and the heart, hand and head choices come together in a single, unified idea, then any choice will be really easy to make. But only by having a clear sense of where you're heading can you be sure that decisions you make today will be of value tomorrow.

Within the know-where-you're-going choice, there are three factors to consider:

- **Distraction disease**. All our journeys start with good intent, but along the way we get sidelined by gifts and goodies, like job titles and thoughts of status, that erode who we are.
- **Bingo ball behaviour**. Often people are allowed to play too great a role in influencing who you are and where you're going.
- **Turn on the potential tap**. When planning where you're going, make sure you draw on your full potential.

Distraction disease

External distractions can knock us off course and make other things seem more attractive than the journey we initially embarked on. These distractions can be power, money, titles or the latest household gadget that you simply must have.

I had made the big step from being a sales support officer to sales manager. The sheer shock, excitement and power that the title gave me was quite staggering. All of a sudden I had the ability to say what was right, decide the fate of people who were 'below' me, and power, oh, power, lead the performance review, when I could sit back and tell people just how much they had upset me all year long.

Then along came the Christmas party, the ideal chance to strut my stuff and display the power badge – a 'new suit'. All was fine until the end of the night. There was a man who was as big as an ox and probably about five times as strong. He'd had more than enough to drink and was getting out of order. After a while he became really agitated and was clearly looking for a fight, so I put on my managerial hat, strolled up to him and, in my most commanding, managerial voice, ordered him to grow up and go home. Feeling pretty proud of myself and having asserted my managerial status to the group, I saw his right fist speeding towards me. At that point, I had a revelation: just because I think I'm a manager it doesn't mean that anyone else does! Luckily, my black eye faded, but the lesson has stuck with me to this day!

If you're trying to calm someone who is drunk and highly agitated, you're dependent on personal power to influence how they see the world through the red mist of alcohol. The whole problem was that I confused who I was with what I did. The figure of Mick Cope The Manager had temporarily obscured the view of Mick Cope The Individual.

Robin Seymour and John Cleese have explored this idea in an excellent book called *Life and How to Survive It*. They consider the notion that people place the role of work over personal life for a number of reasons. First, it gives people a relatively easy way of deriving a sense of purpose rather than having to look at the more personal areas of their lives such as relationships with loved ones. It's far easier to concentrate on the quarterly sales figures or performance targets than to sit down with your partner and openly discuss what you mean to each other, what you believe in and where you want to go in the coming years. Seymour and Cleese also suggest that it helps to structure our time. Rather than having to sit and think, we anxiously rush around looking busy and in the process help ourselves feel important. The downside is that one day the panic stops, we retire or have to slow down, and people can't cope with the freedom, space and time they are offered. It's only when these emotional blinkers are torn off that we realize we've wasted a lot of our life up to that point. The danger is that we let work become more important than life and end up playing a well-known corporate game called 'Whoever has the most toys when they die wins'.

The loss of me

The worrying thing is that this erosion of who I am through the acquisition of what I do is introduced at such an early age.

Take a few minutes to think about when the shift started for you and the route you've taken. What you come up with might be surprising. Compare your results with the list I drew up below, which made me realize just how much I had been sucked in by other people's insecurity magnets. As is often the way, the insecurity pulls seem to grow in strength and number as I get older, and the end result is it becomes even harder to break away from their gravity and take control of my life.

Child	Teenager	Adult	Parent
Drive to acquire toys that are in fashion	Need baggy trousers to look cool	Must renew the car every two years	Must have the right pushchair for the children
Pressure from teacher to climb the ladder table	Must have flowery shirts made by Brutus	Social conditioning to buy house in the right area	Must be able to buy the children the correct computer games
Must have Johnny Seven machine gun (as seen on TV)	Must have alloy wheels on the car (even though they cost more than the car)	Oh no, I don't have a degree: I'm not as good as my manager	Need to ensure that children's friends don't see me driving around in my old Toyota van
	Must have the right haircut	Oh no, I'm getting fat: start the diet treadmill	
	Must have Ben Sherman shirt	Oh my god, the gardening show says we must have decking: quick, buy it and DIY it before the next barbecue	Must have the correct brand label clothes for the teenage children

From an early age we start to trade creativity for compliance, school rules, exam marks, then company games.

Dare to deviate from the norm and you risk losing a bonus or promotion. All the time this is happening, there's a gradual erosion of your personal security and self-reliance, as you replace who you are for what you do.

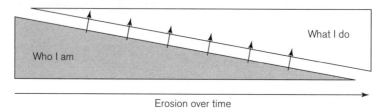

Erosion over time

Figure 2.2   *Who am I? What do I do?*

The end result is often an in-security ramp, indicating the gradual shift during our lives that takes the focus from who we are to what we do. So, over time, we are allowed (and allow ourselves) to spend less time and energy on the inner-self, and instead place greater emphasis on the acquisition of external badges and artefacts. Although we might see a short-term reward in this strategy, we risk giving away control of our lives to other people and things.

True personal leadership must come from the inner strength of who I am, rather than what I do. As you go through life you experience a range of roles, work functions and responsibil-ities. If you changed your personal leadership style every time you moved to a new position you would be like a bingo ball bouncing around yet always under the control of the caller. It's far better to know who we are deep down and use this as the launch pad to drive what we do more effectively.

Knowing where you're going doesn't require a huge project plan or an electronic organizer full of 'to do's'. It's just a clear and succinct idea that indicates who you are and where you're going.

Think of Martin Luther King's famous address. Even in a single sentence he manages to capture the essence of his beliefs, values and dreams – all who listen to or read the address are clear as to his direction:

I have a dream that my four children will one day live in a nation where they will not be judged by the color of their skin but by the content of their character.
I have a dream today.

How would you describe your dreams, beliefs, passion and future goals?

- What are your core values?
- What are your partner's and family's values?
- What do you want to be doing in one, three and five years' time?
- What personal dreams affect the future of your family, friends and work colleagues?
- What will you say 'no' to?
- What are the three things that guide all your important decisions?

Do you have a clear definite response? Test if you truly have a clear outcome by asking your friends, family and peers to answer the same questions about you. If they can give the same answers you gave, then you do know where you're going. If not, then try to define the gap.

Bingo ball behaviour

Think about the last time you were lost on a trip. It might be the overseas holiday when you ventured down a strange street and started to worry for the safety of your family. It might even be the first day of a new job when you started to worry how on earth you would find your way to the toilets. Familiar to each case is a sense of anxiety, confusion and fear of the unknown. You're in a place where there are no directions, guides or help of any kind. Now remember the feeling when you found the first landmark that you recognized. It might be a familiar junction on the freeway, the sound of a church bell or the board room. Whatever the landmark, it's something that gives you a stake in the ground and a basis on which to make a decision. It's this sense of orientation and location that is so important within the personal leadership framework. The ability to find a reference point in times of turmoil and confusion is an essential part of any leadership process.

Think of someone you know who goes through life without any real sense of purpose or direction. It might be that fate is always on hand to offer a guiding hand, but for most of us this isn't the case.

People without purpose have no boundaries, no under-standing of what is good or bad advice, with the result that they respond (and believe) different advice on different days like a bouncing ball in a bingo machine.

Consider the life of Billy, a trainee manager at a large computing company. He is about to attend a promotion interview that could really make a big difference to his income. At the start of the week he has a clear plan to spend his time preparing for next week's interview. However, after a couple of hours Person A comes along and suggests that preparation is of little use because the job is sewn up and will go to someone else. So Billy decides that it's not worth spending time and goes off to do some other work. He then meets B over coffee and she says that the job isn't sewn up at all, they are just looking for someone with a special set of skills. So Billy rushes to the resource centre to track down some reports. At the resource centre, Billy meets an old friend who is also going to be interviewed. They suggest that the

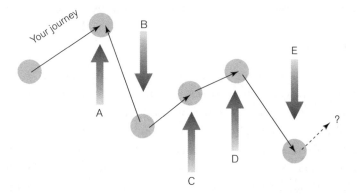

Figure 2.3   *Forces of external advice and requests from other people*

team manager is biased against people with long hair, so Billy rushes out to get a haircut. These diversions continue right up to the interview, and Billy will fail to get the job.

So there we have Bingo Ball Billy, someone who responds to forces from all directions because he doesn't really know where he's going. The alternative is to build a picture that sets out where you're heading and to follow that journey. By setting out the parameters of your journey you can define a corridor or window of opportunity which consists of those things you are prepared to do; everything else falls outside the boundary. For Bingo Ball Billy's next interview, he will need to define who he will listen to, what subjects he will study, who he won't listen to, and what topic areas he will not research. He might go so far as to define what he wants from the job and under what circumstances he will reject any offer.

Your life doesn't have to become unchangeable and set in concrete. As your life circumstances change, you respond and adapt accordingly. But when this happens it's easier to change the operating boundary and be guided by a clear set of principles, rather than trying to make each decision in isolation.

An early experience for me was the decision not to move house. The company I worked for at the time was in reorganization frenzy – every other month there would be a reorganization and accompanying relocation. Around me I could see my colleagues' lives being turned upside down and in some cases relationships being destroyed as they responded to choices made by the company. My choice was not to move my family, but to include the flexibility to travel further to work.

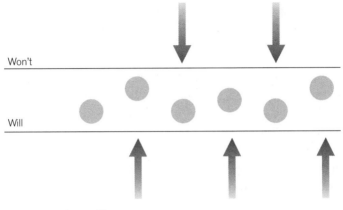

Figure 2.4 *Won't, will*

So, if push came to shove (and it did) I would lodge out for a period to maintain my career but not put my partner and children through the upheaval of moving house and school. Having made this choice, it became very easy to make a career decision. There was no turmoil or tension if promotion came along in an area where I could not commute. It was simply outside the corridor and therefore not an option.

Enter the choice corridor

Once you've defined your choice corridor, it's like having a personal sage or guru on tap 24 hours a day.

Someone you can go to in times of crisis and confusion. A guru who will give you clear considered and practical advice that's guaranteed to help relieve your problem and take away your anxiety and frustration. You get this by having clarity of

Figure 2.5   *Won't, will, won't*

purpose, and knowing where you're going. Once you've put a stake in the ground to say this is where I am and this is where I'm going, you have a starting point of reference, almost like your own global positioning satellite system.

Think about where you are and where you're heading and try constructing your own corridor.

Once you've thought about what you will and won't do, think about the degree of control you have over those factors. Although there are things you're not prepared to do, can you really refuse? Is there a degree of emotional or financial liability to consider, such that you have to abide by someone else's choices? Debt, both moral and financial, often constrains our actions.

So for these choices that you would like to make but can't at the moment because of personal commitment or other liabilities, redraw the corridor, but this time put a timeline along the bottom as in Figure 2.6.

By using the timeline decision corridor you can define what is important now and what might be important in the future. This will help build a richer picture of where you're going and

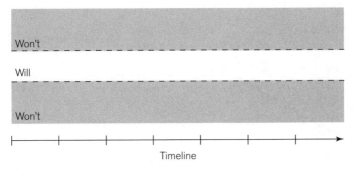

Figure 2.6 *Won't, will, won't and timeline*

what the critical factors are along the way. It might be that some of the 'wills' and 'won'ts' are only aspirations at the moment, but at least they are on the table for you to consider and share with those around you. The final stage in this journey is to take one of the things you wish to achieve, and then ask yourself: How can I make this even better? Take some time to consider your own case.

As an example, you can step up the escalator with me in Figure 2.7. When I worked for a large company, I wanted to develop programmes rather than present other people's ideas; the next stage was to work within the company, running programmes where I had control over the content; leaving to join a company where I could develop and run my own products was the next move; and finally, I left to set up my own company so I could maintain absolute control over the quality and distribution of my ideas. All four steps are different, but they are underpinned both by freedom of choice and my commitment to be with my family.

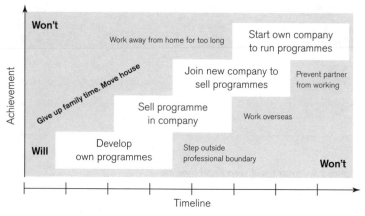

Figure 2.7   *Achievement timeline*

Turn on the potential tap

As you read this book, there will be an inner voice commenting on the ideas, the models, and my typing errors. The voice offers a running commentary on what you're reading and how you think and feel about it, and tries to steer your head and heart in certain directions. In many cases, the inner voice is a powerful tool that helps you fight imaginary monsters or talk yourself through emotional traumas. However, it can also be a tremendously powerful force that prevents you from making real headway in your personal plans. This blocking energy comes from the insecurity driver. This is the part of the heart dimension that believes with absolute passion that there are things in life that you can't do, that will hurt you or that don't make sense. The insecurity driver pushes you to get satisfaction from the things that you know and from others' answers, rather than taking risks yourself.

Think about a sport you play. Most of the time you happily take part in the game and are satisfied with the outcome. But there is probably a certain ball you find difficult to play or a particular player you don't get along with. And every time this thing crops up, your inner voice reminds you. Your inner voice is the little devil in disguise that acts as a potential tap. It's just a tiny voice, but it has the potential to prevent you from releasing the wealth of talent stored in your personal reservoir. However, there are examples of people who have learned to control this inner voice and manage to keep it in line; as a result, they generate more freedom and personal power.

One of the most inspiring stories for me has been that of Christopher Reeve. In a TV interview, Sir David Frost talked with him about the difficulties he faced every day, and asked how he dealt with the shock of not being able to move. Christopher Reeve answered:

I get busy and readjust and focus on what can I do today. There is a phrase that I use which is 'bad days are good days in disguise'. You can start out feeling pretty miserable about the injustice of it all. The way out is to think of something that needs doing and there is always something that will take you forward, and I just focus on that and I get back in shape.

This 'know where you're going' outcome isn't a one-, two- or three-year objective (although that might underpin the overall motivation). Christopher Reeve had to set a new personal outcome the moment he woke up each day. He used this driving force to help him survive the emotional and physical torture he experienced daily. By developing this inner mantra, he used his in-security to overpower the insecurity and was able to prevent negative behaviour from emerging.

The problem is that when trying to define and plan where you're going, the inner voice can set up a raging torrent of critique, all aimed at stopping you from experiencing things that are new and challenging. It might be doing this to protect you, but sometimes it can be wrong. You have to learn to manage it.

'Manage' doesn't mean ignore or overcome.

If you fight it, much of your emotional and intellectual energy is being forced into your internal space, and energy that should be focused on making a change is lost. The trick is to come up with a question to ask the voice. After all, the tap is there to protect you from harm. Like the release valve on a steamer or the governor on an engine, it's being protective in its own way. <u>Rather than fighting the inner voice, set up a series of internal challenges or dialogues</u>. The next time you feel the tap being closed off by the inner voice, ask yourself these questions:

1   What would it be like if I went ahead?

2   What's the worst thing that could happen?

3   What would I do if I weren't afraid?

4   Has anyone else ever done it? What harm came to them?

By using this approach, you're harnessing the intellectual power of the head dimension to challenge some of the fears offered by the insecure part of the heart dimension. By asking these two dimensions to argue their case, it can become possible to overcome irrational fears stimulated by the insecurity driver. It's also important to recognize that, although the logic of the question and argument comes from the head dimension, the energy and passion for this must come from the in-security drive in the heart dimension.

Ultimately, the heart dimension controls the potential tap, and it's this function that controls the release of your potential. Therefore it's important that you understand the importance of the choose-your-choice component. Unless you accept that you have the right, power and energy to manage your internal voices and choices, then all of these words will have little impact.

You just know you're going to hit it this time

The first challenge to set yourself might be to think of one thing that you've always said you can't do. Take this thing that the voice says you can't do and work through the questions shown in Figure 2.8. If they don't fit the issue exactly then bend and shape them to make sense. The primary purpose is to help your head component and the in-security driver to reframe the issue to help the heart understand that it isn't dangerous or life-threatening. If you do a single loop and your heart's answer is still 'no', but the objective has shifted, then circulate again basing your questions on the new objective. Loop as many times as you need to in order to get to a point where your heart is prepared to give it a shot.

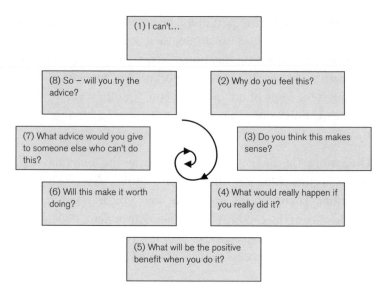

Figure 2.8 *Circulated questions*

1   I can't . . . Think of something you feel you're unable to do. It might be dealing with a problem at work or challenging someone who seems intolerant. Try to focus on something that you know is possible but which seems to have some reason why you can't do it.

2   Why do you feel this? What internal insecurity forces cause you to believe you can't do something? Have you a legacy experience? Or has someone else fed you their fantasy that it's difficult to do?

3   Do you think this makes sense? From a logical perspective why is it a barrier? Is there a sensible reason why you don't want to do it?

4 What would really happen if you went ahead? Just supposing that you did take action, what would happen? What is the worst that could happen? And what is the best?

5 What will the positive benefit be when you do it? Imagine you've taken action. How will your life improve? How will it be better for others and how will this feel for you?

6 Will this make it worth doing? Do the benefits outweigh the pain of making the change? What personal benefits will accrue for you?

7 What advice would you give to someone who can't do this? Step outside your situation. What advice would you give to someone else who is in a similar situation? How would you help them to help themselves?

8 So, will you try the advice? Would you take your own advice and overcome that initial, self-created barrier? When will you effect the change? What's the next barrier you would like to overcome?

To really know where you're going, you need to understand your self-imposed limitations and work out ways to overcome them. If you do what you always did, you will get what you always got. Unless you really believe that you have your personal leadership in place and don't need to change, you will benefit by changing your entrenched ideas and habits. Even if you believe that you don't need to change how you operate, it will pay to challenge that assumption!

Avoid crashing at bluffers' bend

A word of warning. I've seen so many people going through their goal-setting process who come out with wild statements that bear little resemblance to what they are or what they might be. The rule is to be true to yourself and be true to others. Don't think you can go for gold in the high jump at the Olympics if you're 47 years old and weigh 19 stone. You might be willing to try, but the drain on your life would be quite devastating. There is little joy in seeing someone giving everything up to achieve an impossible dream. The heart will let you fly but the head will always ensure you don't have a bumpy landing. While hope plays a great part in our lives, realism often takes over to keep pain and misery to a minimum; having outlandish expectations can be emotionally destructive, especially for our loved ones. And be genuine with others. Falsifying your future will destroy your credibility and, even worse, can destroy the good will and trust that you need to call on in order to achieve your true goals in life.

Know where you are going – the three levels

Leader of leaders	**Lead leaders** – Seek to create a rich understanding of the overall direction – one that is inclusive of all the leaders' needs and not exclusive to yours.
Leader of others	**Lead others** – Create and share a directional statement that helps others to follow where you are heading without confusion.
Leader of self	**Lead yourself** – Ensure you are clear as to where you are going and have the ability to share it succinctly with others.

Know where you're going: quick summary

1 You have three aspects to your life: the way you behave – the part others see; the way you think – the rational part of you; the way you feel – your secret inner life that only you know. When these are separated, you feel confused or anxious; when aligned, you gain a clear sense of purpose.

2 Problems occur when you: say you'll take one journey but want to take another; don't know what journey you want to take; take opposing journeys to those with whom you work or live.

3 Having a clear sense of where you're heading ensures that the choices you make today will be of value tomorrow.

4 Who you are and what you do are two very different entities – confuse them at your peril. Don't become so dependent on a person or group that they become your primary source of personal power or income.

5 Imagine what you'd be able to achieve if you weren't afraid of that first step. Challenge the inner voice that's blocking your potential tap. Move from 'I can't' to 'I can'.

6 Map your personal inventory so you understand where your strengths and weaknesses are and how they can best be deployed.

7 Avoid the New Year's resolution situation where personal promises fail to materialize – define where you're going and ensure you have the will and capability to get there.

map your map

The man who views the world at 50 the same as he did
at 20 has wasted 30 years of his life.

Muhammad Ali

THINK ABOUT where you are at the moment. Are you able to step back and take a view of the world as it is rather than how you think you see it? Do you see other people's points of view and accept them as reasonable? Are you able to step outside any entrenched view of yourself and others and take a fresh look at who you are and what you want to be? Maybe you believe that you are able to look at every situation afresh, but for the most part people have slipped into a singular and biased way of looking at themselves and others without ever realizing it.

Imagine your plane is coming in to land at Heathrow airport, and suddenly the pilot announces that the undercarriage is stuck and the plane will have to make an emergency landing. When the plane lands, you're instructed to leave the plane rapidly, as a fire may break out. Do you leave quickly and safely as instructed, or, as is the reality in many crashes, do you put your life at risk by waiting to get your things out of the overhead luggage rack?

Most people still follow the mental map programmed for a normal landing. The standard map is, on landing, everyone stands up and waits to get their possessions, and only once this task is achieved do they leave the plane. In an emergency, however, speed is of the essence, and the quickest person out of the plane has the greatest chance of survival. Evidence suggests that those who survive are the people who ignore the existing map of self-imposed rules, and look for ways to circumvent the normal landing procedures. They do this by increasing the level of variety in the maps used to make sense of the world.

Rich variety: get spoilt for choice

We need to always have sufficient variety to generate new ideas and look at ourselves and the world in new and fresh ways. This approach is known as Ashby's law of requisite variety. Ross Ashby suggested that any regulator must have as much or more variety than the system it regulates. In a game of chess, the variety of moves you have available must be greater than the variety of moves available to your opponent. The same can be seen in football, the stock market or a children's painting competition. In any situation, you have to understand how much choice and variety exists, and then be able to match or exceed this level. The person with the most flexibility will influence and lead the environment.

Think back to when you were a child, desperate for the latest toy. You wanted it badly. It was the most important thing in the world. But your mum refused, so you went to your dad. He in turn refused, so you pressured your grandparents and favourite aunties and uncles. After this failed to work you adopted different strategies: sulking, sobbing, screaming and scratching the brand new furniture. This went on and on until your strategies worked. Even though the grown-ups tried to respond to all your strategies with their own responses, ultimately you outdid them. You had the staying power to try more and more ways to get want you wanted from them. As a parent, there are only so many punishments you can invoke, but as a child the options available are mind blowing. At this point both you and your parents experienced the awesome power of rich variety.

Your persistence can be summarized as 'if what you're doing doesn't work, do something else'. The head dimension uses this as its primary ethos and argues that we must increase the variety of ways in which we lead ourselves and others. We use the variety in two ways. First, we use the diversity to see life from more than just a unitary standpoint. Second, life is movement and movement is change. If we are to change ourselves and others successfully, we must learn how to map our maps and change how we change.

To enhance your personal leadership you have to look beyond the standard solutions and learn how to originate new ideas and alternatives. The person who has only restricted variety in their armoury will fall by the wayside as other competitors come along and offer more diverse, rich and imaginative solutions.

Restricted variety

So, how do we know when a person, team or organization has a restricted mental map? Think of the typical political interview. The pattern is generally consistent. The politician is asked a question by the interviewer and promptly responds with a pre-planned monologue of what they believe is right or wrong about the current situation. The answer might well be very interesting, but the interviewer wants to broaden the discussion, so asks another question. The politician responds but gives pretty much the same information as before, perhaps framed slightly differently. So the charade goes on, with the interviewer in the guise of attacker and the guest acting as valiant defender, persistently rehashing the same idea.

Whenever human beings come together in a group, they instinctively create a framework for restrictive variety. If you accept the premise that maximized variety is better than minimized variety, ask yourself why we don't do more of it.

In its natural state, the world is a cauldron of natural richness and variety. In their natural state, human beings are infinitely variable – two people are never totally the same. Put these two sets of variables together and we have a world that is complex and chaotic. To survive in this world we have to filter out a great deal of randomness and create mental maps that bring order and common sense into our lives. In effect, we choose the degree of variety required to make life liveable. As we are continually trying to bring order into our lives by restricting the variety we face, when we form into groups or make associations, the restrictive process is compounded.

The average level of mediocrity! (ALOM)

This standardizing or restricting of options and choices results in the average level of mediocrity. Put together a football team of highly talented players, and the restrictive factors actually clash and constrain the talent within the group. So one player's preferred style might be to run down the wing and cross a high ball for someone to head in from inside the box, while the centre-forward's preference is to avoid heading the ball, preferring to work through the back line with one-on-one tackling.

The football manager's role is partly about getting skilled players into the team but, more importantly, being able to recognize where restrictive forces will reduce the overall effectiveness of the team.

The ALOM effect can be seen in any situation where two or more people come together. In an organization, it will be evident in everything the organization says and does. Every time it puts in a new process or system it imposes the mental map of the designer on the organization and those using the system, and prevents them from using their own unique thoughts, feelings and behaviours. The leader's view of the world places you in a position of restricted behaviour.

Take any system, process, standard, project methodology. They all limit and constrain the level of variety. But with good reason – any business that wants to deliver the right product, to the right person, at the right time, at the right cost, must control its processes to maintain consistency. However, controls over the way the business behaves shouldn't mean that they restrict the way people feel and think.

The strange thing about ALOM is that it's not something obvious that you notice when you walk into an organization. As a consultant I can visit an organization and the president will proudly tell me of their work rate, staff survey records and key performance measures. This tells me what they are doing well, but it doesn't tell me what they could be doing better. Whenever I consult with a company I always try to ask one simple question. 'On a scale of 0–10 [10 being the most positive] to what degree does the organization unleash and tap into the potential of its people?' The average score is between 3 and 5. In some cases I get a 7, but in others it drops to 0 and 1. When I ask this question, it isn't just to the workers and frontline operators, I ask the same question throughout the business, and the result is consistent, even in companies known to be innovative leaders in work style and performance.

In order to lead others effectively you must have the ability to unleash the latent and innate talent that lies untouched throughout most people's working lives. Don't let your team members be like Marlon Brando in *On the Waterfront*: 'I could have been a contender.' Personal leadership is about never saying 'I could have . . .', it's about saying 'I have'.

Remapping our maps

In this section, we'll look at the following:

1   Map shift. The world moves on at such a pace that we need to discard our old view and take on board a whole new set of feelings, thoughts and behaviours.

2   Map conflict. In the main, conflict doesn't occur because of a problem, it's just that two people are viewing the same situation from a different perspective. Build a bridge

between the two maps and the potential for conflict is reduced.

3 Fantasy ladder. Our mental maps are not rigid and they become distorted over time. What appears to be the truth or a correct decision one day might seem totally different another day. This distortion happens as we turn fact into fantasy through inference.

4 Map expansion. One way to enrich your map is to explore other people's maps. As the two views contrast, conflict and coalesce, you can create a new view of the world that is unique and full of possibilities.

Map shift

The root of all leadership and learning is the map shift, where an individual has to be prepared to discard or throw away the current world view and accept an alternative frame of reference. In making this shift, the self-sustaining loop must be broken. This loop is a common process; people see the world in a particular way, and so expect it to behave according to the criteria set out in their own particular mental map. For you to change yourself or others you must create a break in the current pattern and force a shift to a new way of thinking (see Figure 3.1).

Once the world is seen in a new way, the shift can be used to reinforce this new world position. However, this can soon drift towards the negative. If you decide to stop at that point, and don't use the experience to energize further map shifts, then the change or learning will only be of limited value.

Reinforcing loop

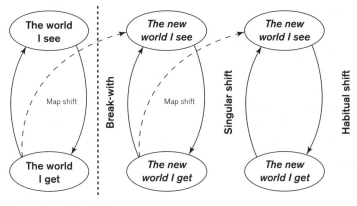

Figure 3.1 *Map shift*

Failure to change mapping rarely has extreme consequences but the failure of the commanding officers to accept that the invasion of Singapore in 1941 would occur at the site where it did resulted in the death of thousands of people. Defences were designed on the assumption that any invasion would be sea-based and would come from the southern side of the island. As a result, the northern shore was left undefended. Although the local plantation owners, who understood the Malay Peninsula and the Japanese people, repeatedly highlighted the risk of attack from the north, they were overruled or ignored by the commanding forces. And even when Japanese transports were sighted off the southern tip of Indo-China, the potential for a northern attack was negated.

The problem was rooted in the fact that the guardians of Singapore could not risk allow themselves to be wrong and routinely issued communiqués to the people of Singapore denying that a problem existed. Only in 1948 did General

Wavell admit to the governor of Singapore that the fault for the lack of preparation must be placed on the heads of the military. You can see how the cause of the problem must have arisen from an inability and unwillingness among the leaders to free themselves from their entrenched ways of thinking and accept that alternatives might be available.

Once you break with the past, you can create the future you desire, and the idea of true personal leadership, where you control your own life, can start to emerge. First you learn to understand the boundaries we all operate within and then you begin to understand how to stretch your own boundaries every day. We all have personal limitations that are imposed by us, by external factors, or jointly. These are the maps that we operate with. If I have a map of the London Underground, I can find my way around London by tube; if I have a map of the world, my choice is boundless.

Map conflict

Problems can arise when people 'believe' they are operating with the same map – whereas in reality they are worlds apart. Shortly after I met my wife, she was working away and had decided to stay at my cousin's house in a small village called Bourne End. Although she had visited the house a couple of times, both times I had driven us there. Anyway, she felt confident enough about getting there and, at the end of her day's work, drove off to Bourne End and started to look for my cousin's house. She drove around for ages but couldn't seem to spot any useful landmarks. After a while she telephoned me and I tried to give her directions over the phone. All seemed OK – she knew that she had to look for a garage and then the house was a short way down on the left-hand side. After another half an hour she telephoned me again – she couldn't find it. Although I was trying to understand her problem, it was getting late and I was tired and (in so many words) just told her to open her eyes and look for it, after all there was only one garage in the village! Then, at last, after more heated phone calls, we realized she was in the wrong Bourne End!

So, I had been giving her directions based on my mental map, and she had been trying to apply them to the (totally mismatched) territory in front of her.

Map gap

My own experience has taught me:

- We often make assumptions about the map we use in relation to the maps other people use – this can lead to map dissonance or a difference in your respective views of the world.

- It's easy to fall into the trap that the map is the territory – clearly, the map is a representation of a physical set of characteristics, not the actual thing.

- The power of positive thinking means nothing at all if you're in the wrong place.

In essence the gaps between what we see and what others see leads to map gap, a dissonance between our reality and someone else's. You know the situation: we both go to see a film. I come out saying how great it was, especially the bit where the spy jumped from one building to another in the howling winds. You say what a load of rubbish and how can a person jump 25 feet in torrential winds. We've both experienced the same event but choose to create alternative, and conflicting, maps.

The key word I use here is choose.

We've both experienced the same event, at the same time, in the same place, and you'd expect that we'd end up with the same inner descriptions. But this clearly didn't happen. What does happen is that we tend to choose to selectively filter the film through the maps we already have. I could have chosen to view the 25-foot jump as false and theatrical, but my map was one of: 'I'm here to enjoy myself and switch my brain off for two hours. I don't want to analyze and compare things; I just want an emotional, thrilling experience.' Your map is probably more head-based. You went to the movies for stimulation and were intuitively analyzing the film to see how it stacked up against reality. However, we both had choices about how we view the film. I could have gone with a different emotion in place, used a different map and had a totally different experience.

It's this inner choice that leads to shared decisions to build empires, pyramids and political systems. But it's the same inner choice that causes conflict. Look in any newspaper the world over and I guarantee that up to 50 per cent of the stories are based on the idea of map dissonance. Where one party disagrees with another; one lobby group frames an argument in an alternate way to another; or one aspiring political leader presents an alternative approach to the other candidate.

Map versus territory

However, all of these presentations are positional representations – they are not the truth! Any map we hold in our head is representation of the territory. It can never be the real thing because it isn't the real thing. If you want to know what it feels like to walk across the Sahara desert, then you have to do it. Reading a book on North Africa simply won't give you access to that experience.

What we see in our heads isn't what exists. Unfortunately, people believe that their internal representation is the territory. They believe that their understanding is the truth and that no other variation can exist. Take a look at any form of extremism. Apartheid, fascism, religious cults, even football hooliganism, are based on the premise that theirs is the only answer (or football team). Where such dogma exists it becomes difficult to build bridges and develop any sense of shared success.

Exposing the person to the facts, as they exist and as perceived by other people, is one way of achieving this. My insistence that I was giving the right directions to Bourne End was only pulled short when Lin found out that actually there are two Bourne Ends. Now, I could have disagreed with that, but in reality, once she pointed it out then I could understand the problem. We sometimes have to go through this process to help people with entrenched beliefs step outside themselves for a while and see the world from a different perspective.

The acceptable truth

Making a shift in our personal maps requires accepting another person's truth. There's often a tendency for the inner voice to chirp away in the background offering a running commentary on the world. As we watch news broadcasts, read the paper or listen to people talk, a switch toggles between 'I agree' and 'I disagree'. We do this without even realizing what the inner voice is doing, but it can have a powerful impact on how we act and respond in different situations. Just reading this paragraph, your inner voice will have said 'yes, that's right', or prompted you to feel irritated at the fact that someone else asserted that you don't have logical control over how you behave.

The difference between what you find acceptable and unacceptable can be quite straightforward like 'I don't like the taste of whisky', or it might be a more subtle preference where you happen to prefer a certain type of whisky. It might be difficult to separate acceptable from unacceptable where the separation is unclear, and, of course, preferences can change from day to day, but it's important to have some under-standing of where your preferences lie on the acceptability line (Figure 3.2) and what they mean to you, because ultimately this delineation drives the choices you make.

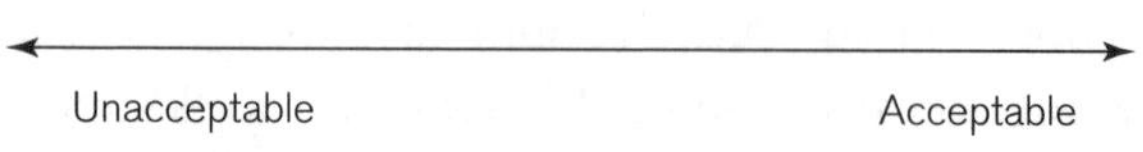

Unacceptable   Acceptable

Figure 3.2   *Acceptability line*

I find this...

Unacceptable	Acceptable

Figure 3.3 *I find this ...*

UA maps

One of the important aspects of the 'map your map' choice and the head dimension is to understand and map some of your unacceptable and acceptable (UA) preferences (see Figure 3.3). Just think about it. To what extent do you know what you know? How successfully could you sit down and describe 'you' to someone else in terms of your preferences? I'm sure you could gleefully list your partner's, friends' or boss's UA preferences, but when it comes to your own it can be quite difficult. Why not give it a try? Don't just go for the obvious ones, try to look at some of the deeper aspects that really drive how you think, feel and behave. For example, how do you feel about eating meat, fox hunting, children who scream in restaurants, dog lovers who don't scoop the poop, kids who get drunk in your town on a Friday night, or the use of chlorine in the water system? Try to think of the many judgements your inner voice makes.

When I had to hit the deadline for this book, I decided to go away on my own for a week and leave the trials and tribulations of family life behind me. I called into the travel agents and booked the first cheap holiday that I could get that was guaranteed to get me some sun. While writing this section, I just stopped for a while and watched life go on around me, but I also listened to my inner voice rattling away as it offered comments on the passing world. It was an enlightening and powerful experience. In the space of ten minutes my inner voice passed comments on:

- hotels that leave open bottles of vodka next to the children's bowl of orange
- children allowed to run by the pool where it's slippery
- the check-out time for the last day
- being in an all-English hotel
- women sunbathing topless
- Minorca in comparison to Malta
- the wisdom of eating meat.

For all of these fleeting thoughts, there was ultimately a UA decision being made and filed away as a frame of reference for the future. While I'm conscious of these processes and UA allocation, I can step back and challenge the inner voice forming the inner maps. This is part of the rationale for building your UA map. Just by writing from the heart, rather than from the head, you can start to understand how you frame life, what causes you to make decisions, and which of your UA preferences you're happiest with. By mapping how you map, you can start to choose how you might like your map to look.

While you're mapping your map, it might be useful to understand how other people map their UA preferences. Just what do other people find acceptable and unacceptable? Why? And how do their UA maps differ from yours? Think of one person you find it difficult to get along with. Picture them clearly in your mind and start to think about how they think, feel and behave. Try to write down what their UA map looks like.

Consider how much your map differs from theirs. If you can find things that are significantly different, try to think about

They find this...

Unacceptable	Acceptable

Figure 3.4   *They find this ...*

the gap. What is it that's different? If the head map indicates that you are opposites, what in the heart is driving this? Do you have opposite values in life or do you share any likes and dislikes?

Comparative mapping can help you understand the differences between you and the important people in your life.

Take five minutes to draw a UA map for someone you get along with really well (see Figure 3.5).

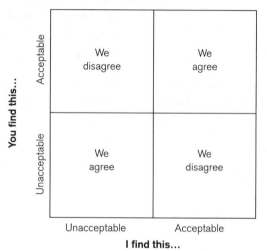

Figure 3.5 *UA map*

You'll find that whether you like or dislike a person, your maps will never agree. We all have our own maps, they're all different, and none of them is the 'right' one.

Use the UA map to:

● understand your UA preferences

● choose those you wish to keep

- choose those you'll change and choose what the change will be
- understand other people's UA maps and accept that they are just that, maps, not truths
- start to understand how to build bridges and work in a more effective way with other people.

To lead yourself and others effectively, you must disregard observed behaviour and, instead, start to understand what maps are being used to drive behaviour. If you meet someone you perceive to be stand-offish and withdrawn, ignore that and start to understand what it is that drives that behaviour. You might also start to question where your judgement of their behaviour comes from. I don't know anyone who says they're stand-offish and withdrawn, but I do know lots of people who like to have private space and prefer to get closer to people over a longer time frame than others. Rather than them being distant, it might be that you have certain drivers in your unacceptable frame that cause you to be averse to such behaviour.

UA patterns

The UA map can help us further to develop understanding of conversation and behaviour. It highlights the following:

- the boring band
- the possibility band
- loop mapping.

The boring band is so called because there's a good chance that two people operating from these maps will tend to rehash old ideas and discussions rather than being generative in their approach. Consider Figure 3.6, where you have groups of people who share similar maps on what is acceptable and unacceptable. There is a chance they will simply agree on everything and agree to disagree on things they don't agree on. This is not to suggest that people who share similar UA maps will never be creative, but any creativity is likely to be bounded within the maps that already exist.

Contrasting the pattern in Figure 3.7, with the possibility band there is a good chance that sparks will fly and new ideas will be created from the fusion of these minds. People with different UA maps will walk into areas they might have deemed wrong in relation to their personal domain. The power of possibility within this band comes not necessarily from the heat of the disagreement, but more when they know

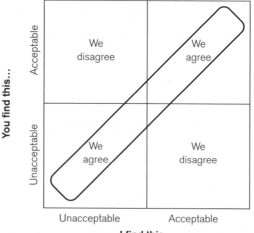

Figure 3.6   UA patterns

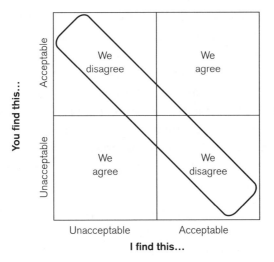

Figure 3.7   *UA patterns*

and accept that they have different maps, and that that's precisely why they've come together.

For example, if sales of a product are falling, the response from people operating in the boring band might be to alter the promotional discount, increase the number of outlets, or in extreme cases sack the product manager. For people in the possibility band, they will adopt a more generative approach and challenge each other to think about some of the broader problems. They might ask richer questions about the falling sales of a product. To what extent is there conflict in the marketplace with other products the company sells? Are cross-portfolio problems emerging? Has research and development lagged so that the product has become dated? Are the sales performance targets at odds with the needs of the product turnover levels?

The key to the possibility band is in the art of turning the questions back on themselves through the use of shared dissonance to create new options and possibilities. They would ask what underlying assumptions are being made, and what the values of the questioner are in suggesting that a problem exists in the first place. For example, instead of a manager trying to determine why the performance of a team member has fallen, they might ask themselves why it took so long to notice, or what steps are being taken to develop all the individuals in the team.

The possibility band is a place where new and original ideas come to the fore – a metaphor that describes the areas that people can go to, but normally prefer to avoid. Often when exploring new ways of working or thinking, arbitrary and self-imposed constraints exist that prevent people and organizations from tackling normal problems in new and innovative ways. There can be a tendency to stick with the knitting, play safe and stay inside the comfort zone. Even worse is the desire to keep other people in their comfort zone. By fusing people together who don't agree, it's possible to create new shared maps that exceed the breadth and depth of the current ones.

The final pattern is loop mapping, where energy and ideas are wasted because a group of people, all with different maps, compete against each other rather than create new options.

In a team environment, if you get to a point where map blockage has occurred, it helps to set a rolling pattern within the team (see Figure 3.8). Starting in the 'Let's agree' box, find

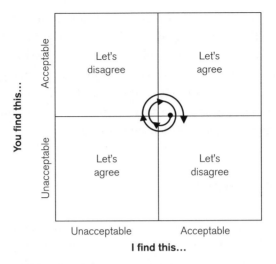

Figure 3.8 *Loop mapping*

something that you all agree on. Once the team is at ease, move to the 'Let's disagree' box, where you have the chance to present your own views and ideas on what's right and see how they differ from other people's. Give the team the freedom to critique your assumptions and help realign your map. Move on to 'Let's agree what we don't find acceptable' to define the outer boundary of the group, and, finally, go on to what you find unacceptable, and others are happy with. Try to understand why the difference is there and how it might be used to create new options.

Keep following this loop pattern until you're able to accept the other people's maps and hopefully have stretched the total map of the group to new levels. Loop mapping is hugely beneficial because it avoids the traditional confrontation and battle-based approach to group working and introduces a sweeping style that is inclusive but still challenging and dynamic. The underlying dynamic is a give–get orientation. At one point you might be giving your UA map to others, and then five minutes later you're in an inquiry state, trying to get from them how they view the world. The energy and synthesis of this interaction creates a new generative model of group working that is stretching but safe.

Fantasy ladder

Our mental maps are not rigid but this means they can become distorted over time and what appears to be the truth or a correct decision one day might appear totally different on another day. This distortion can be almost imperceptible and is driven by many factors, including personal values, political forces, fears or simple forgetfulness. The shift from hard, objective data to subjective fiction can quite rapidly take you through a number of stages (see Figure 3.9), based on the ladder of inference developed by Chris Argyris:

- I see something happen that is quite factual

- I select details from what I observe, based on my beliefs and values

- I use these details and add my personal meanings, based on personal experiences

- this view shifts from interpretation to hard fact

- I take actions and change my behaviour, based on these new beliefs.

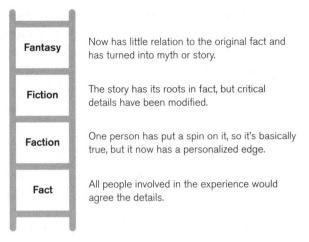

Figure 3.9 *Personal fantasy ladder*

At the bottom of the ladder is a fact or event that happens to you. You select elements of the event and turn it into faction, something that is basically true but is influenced and modified by our map of the world. The faction turns into fiction, as the biased story is translated into a distorted view of what happened – although some element of the fact can be found, you would have to dig quite deep to uncover the real events. Finally, the fiction turns into fantasy as the story takes on mythical status. This may be triggered by the original fact, but has nothing to do with it in terms of either content or detail.

This happens all the time in the political arena. A new and reputable politician gets elected to Parliament. They build a reputation as a good politician and an honest broker. But in a television interview they make a comment that seems to contradict statements made in an earlier campaign. People start to mistrust the politician and this links readily with the stereotypical view of politicians who make promises and break them. The politician is branded a liar and manipulator and further tales get them deselected at the earliest opportunity. What was a slight shift in political position becomes a radical turn around in political posture.

Personal fantasy ladder

The climb up the fantasy ladder doesn't have to involve other people. This is something that you do individually, and often in seconds. Think about the last time you made a presentation to an audience. All's going well until you realize that the man at the end of the third row is not paying attention. As you look more closely you realize that he is actually typing away on his laptop. Immediately, the insecurity driver kicks in, and you think that your presentation is failing. You start to climb up to the faction level as you conclude that other people are probably not interested either and are just looking interested to be polite. Then you reach the fiction stage where you believe that your presentational style is all wrong. You're not clever enough, you look like a mess and don't have any funny stories to draw upon like the really good presenters. By the end, you've made a headlong jump into fantasy and decided that you'll never do any more of this type of presentation – you're not up to it and it's far better coming from someone who knows what they're doing.

This leap up the ladder is a common event and one that people torment themselves with on a daily basis. If not during a presentation then it might be how you react in a team meeting, at a family gathering or at college. The point is that we often climb the ladder without any real need to. We let the insecurity and restricted variety drivers build conclusions about us and others that are unclear or totally false. In the case of the presentation, it might have been that the man at the end of the row was really enthused about your presentation and wanted to capture all the elements that weren't in the overheads.

Unless you take time to climb down the ladder and operate at fact level, you'll be forever operating in fantasy land.

Shared fantasy ladder

Imagine you've had an argument with someone at work. Although it's a silly spat that you manage to resolve, you can see how it starts to make its way up the fantasy ladder. At the time both you and the other person might be able to describe what happened, and your descriptions would match closely enough. But just moments after it happens, you call a close colleague and describe the argument to them. You put small, personal spins on the situation so, at the second level, your description is still true, but your personal embellishments have turned it into faction. Your friend will meet others at work and tell them what happened, but this time they put their own spin on the situation. At this point the story takes a leap from faction to fiction. The event being described, though recognizable, is now different. Your friend wants to enhance your position and the story is increasingly focused on what you did right and what the other person did wrong. So much of the truth has been replaced with distorted information. Finally, the word gets around about what happened and the tale takes on enormous changes as more and more personal views are added in. The original event becomes a fantasy that has very little to do with fact. But remember, both sides of the story have climbed the fantasy ladder and we can see how a gap or canyon can emerge in the relationship (see Figure 3.10).

Fantasy provides the potential for conflict. The escalation from fact to fantasy leads to conflict at home, at work, on the sports field, and even to wars between nations. Take any major conflict and it's generally possible to trace back each side's story to a root fact or incident. The irony is that once the fantasy is built on each side, the conflict is no longer about anything substantial – it's simply about egos, beliefs, political position and power.

Some fissures are only small and the fantasy gap can be resolved by climbing down the ladder and re-agreeing the real facts. However, a fissure can split so far that the conflict starts to cause a real problem. And, once the fantasy story is public and in place, it can be hard for both sides to climb down the ladder to talk about the real rather than the fictitious issue.

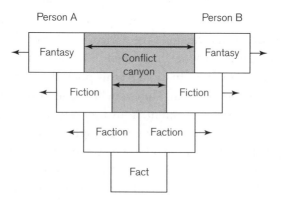

Figure 3.10 *Conflict canyon*

Fantasy forces

This type of reframing can be seen in the home as we make distinctions between right and wrong based on our relationships with other family members. When I was a teenager and lived with my parents, the house we lived in wasn't a big place and, as the lounge was small, we didn't have a lot of space. When the dinner table was set up, it used to be quite difficult to find a free space to put your tea cup or soft drink. One day I walked into the lounge and didn't see the coffee cup that my mother had put down on the floor next to her chair. Within a second the coffee was all over the carpet and we were rushing around trying to get a cloth to mop it up before the coffee stained. At the time my dad chewed me out for being careless and not looking where I was going. Fair enough, I thought, he was right, it was my fault. The next day, as I crashed out to watch the wrestling on a Saturday afternoon, I put the cup on the floor next to my chair. In walked my mother who promptly sent the cup flying, and yet again we scrabbled to find a cloth to mop the tea up before it stained the carpet. Now dad chewed me out for putting the cup on the floor. I couldn't believe it! I tried to tell him how unfair he was being, but to no avail, he was in full flow and nothing was going to stop him.

I believe that my dad's natural intuition to defend mum led him to form decisions in each instance as to what had happened and who was to blame. In both cases he passionately believed that he was right. This is because he was influenced by the legacy of his relationships with us all (mine was that I was a slob and left rubbish all over the place) and his personal values and beliefs (see Figure 3.11). These were

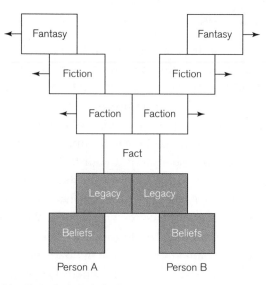

Figure 3.11 *From fantasy to fact*

driven by his love of my mother and a natural desire to support her. She had the job of running the household and none of us was much good at helping her. So although the facts were broadly the same, he formed a rapid interpretation based on what he believed and what had happened in the past.

The question is, to what extent do you do the same? If you have a problem with a team member or co-worker, do you try to stay at the fact level and deal with the problem based upon what happens? Or do you build on your past relationship with your colleague and race up the ladder, and end up trying to resolve a fantasy problem?

From fantasy to fact

Ultimately, the only way down conflict canyon is through the use of productive conversations. These are conversations that help tackle underlying issues that sit beneath the words we use when talking. The first point is to agree that there is a difference of viewpoint. Once this is agreed, we have a safe way to stop the fissure in its tracks and we can ask several questions:

● What are the observable facts that drive the statements being made?

● Do we both agree on the facts as offered?

● Can you run me through your viewpoint and why you believe certain things?

● How did we get from those facts to the current situation?

● What difference do you see between my view of the situation and yours?

● Will you let me try to understand why you feel this way about the issue?

● What is important to you personally?

These questions are used to specifically climb down the ladder and drop below fact level, to understand the person, rather than just the situation.

As you try to understand the deeper issues, there are two areas to consider:

● What are the legacy choices that you and the other person have made in the past that impact on the issue? What is your history together and is this history a factor that will prevent you from having a productive relationship?

- Do you understand the beliefs and values that are important to the person and which have an impact on the creation of any fantasy ladder?

In the majority of cases, the climb up the fantasy ladder is driven by deep-rooted personal values and beliefs rather than the specifics of the circumstances. Only when the legacy and values are understood can you stand any chance of moving down the fantasy ladder to deal with the fact of the problem.

The football manager who constantly argues with one of the star players is actually fighting a beliefs battle, where he believes that the manager has to operate a firm command and control regime, whereas the footballer believes that the effective sportsperson has to be free in order to release their talent.

Admittedly, this type of productive conversation is rarely easy. Even the simplest question about how someone else views their world can feel like a challenge to their beliefs. If you really want to step down and operate at fact level, one approach is to operate from a position of disclosure first, inquiry second and advocacy third. In this way, once you display that you're prepared to share your framework, then understand another person's world view, it becomes easier to understand how their frame might not fit with the leadership frame you're trying to install.

Who mapped your map?

The problem with the fantasy ladder is that maps can be based on 'facts' which are actually fantasy. Every day tabloid myths are perpetuated because people believe what they read. On a grander scale a whole nation can turn fact into fantasy. A child reared in an environment where, for example, racial discrimination is accepted, or even favoured, might know deep down that lies and falsehoods have been spun in order to ensure a certain form of political power is maintained. And the titans of corporate concerns, media moguls and political parties employ large teams just to manage people's maps. If you take one step back and map your map of the world, how much of it is built on fact, and how much is based on fantasy? And how do you know the difference between the two?

What filters and tests can you apply to ensure you're not being fed information that's clouded with fictional additions by those who have played with the ideas? For example, how do you know if the latest story from your chairperson is fact, faction, fiction or fantasy? To what extent are you confident that the feedback you received at your last appraisal wasn't clouded? It's the transfer of one person's fantasy to another's fact that leads to grapevine growth in organizations (see Figure 3.12). Person A is at a meeting where the director briefs the team about a new pay scheme that will be due next year. But they push it up the ladder and believe that the new pay scheme is actually designed to cut the overall pay budget. Person A tells B, B turns it into a belief that the pay budget must be cut because the business is in trouble, and in effect, they now believe that the company has major financial problems and might be looking to make people redundant. B tells C this story and C infers a new fantasy that job cuts are imminent. All these people are receiving other people's

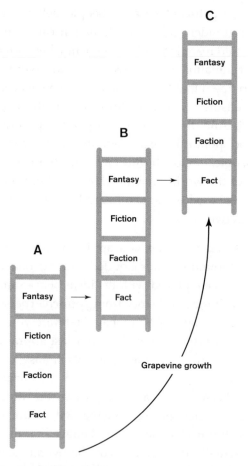

Figure 3.12   *Grapevine growth*

fantasies and have little appreciation of the real facts of the matter.

Think about the headings below. Consider how you would describe your beliefs on each one:

- the political situation in this country
- the current economic situation
- the extent to which religious integration should be encouraged
- the extent to which gay sex should be more openly discussed.

Once you've considered your views on each of these topics, ask yourself:

- Do I trust my information sources not to have pushed the details up the fantasy ladder?
- Do I trust their sources not to have pushed the information up the ladder?
- Do I make time to read opposing views to counterbalance the current map and test where my views are on the ladder?
- Am I confident that my current map of the world is unbiased and free of fantasy contamination?

If you can answer 'Yes' to these questions, your map is no doubt pristine, accurate and unbounded – congratulations! But be careful. You may have developed the ability to see the world as it is and acquire rich variety in the way you view life, but I'm sure that most racist and bigoted political parties have such a view. It's far better to believe that your view is biased and corrupted, then you'll always seek to test and validate your map of the world, rather than sitting back on the assumption that you've got it right.

Throughout the process of mapping your map you should create opportunities wherever you can to enrich your variety, and avoid accepting other people's views of the world. If you choose not to review your map and to stick with your current version, you've locked yourself into a kind of self-imprisonment. This can only ever limit your opportunity to lead yourself and others in a more effective way. Your map has to be flexible.

If you see beauty in art and I see paint then I lose. If you see the sunrise in the morning and I hear the dogs barking, then I lose. If you see market opportunities and I see market problems, then I lose. We all have the freedom to see the world as we wish to see it or as others see it. The important thing is to choose the choice and not fritter it away through apprehension or apathy.

Map expansion

One way to enrich your variety is to seek out, map and explore other people's maps. As the two views contrast, conflict and coalesce, you can create a new view of the world that is unique and full of possibilities. Only by appreciating how people who work with you see their experiences can you hope to share sustainable and profitable relationships with them.

One way to do this is by using the framework shown in Figure 3.13. There are a number of ways to look at the world, but in essence they all boil down to 'my view' and 'your view', where the 'you' includes everyone else apart from 'me'. At the moment there are maps that I have of the world that make

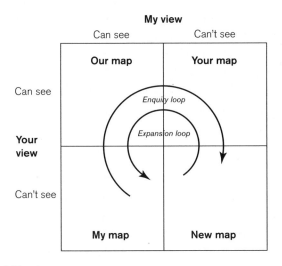

Figure 3.13 *Journey map*

sense and there are things in the world that I can't see. The map enquiry matrix suggests that I might undertake two journeys of discovery.

The first is to start from a view of the world that is essentially my map. This is a view that I have but that you don't see.

I then start on an journey of enquiry to understand how you view the world that we both operate in. At this point I am in the 'our map' segment. From there I can enquire how you look at life in areas that I've never experienced. At this stage we both understand the world we share and the world outside our boundaries. We have created a new map for ourselves, one that has more variety than when we started.

Once we understand the differences between our two maps, we can start the expansion journey. I can start to pull your experiences, values and maps into my view of the world. I can try to understand the points of view that differ from mine and then assimilate them into my frame of reference. At the end of the journey I've arrived back at the 'my map' quadrant, though now I have a broader, richer and deeper understanding of how you see the world and therefore richer variety within my own map.

As the revised map enquiry matrix in Figure 3.14 shows, at the end of the expansion and assimilation process we have both increased the size of 'our map' so the 'our map' quadrant has now increased in size, ideally by more than a factor of two. The process of enquiry and assimilation should not be a doubling process. If effective, it will prove to be a compound exercise where the synergies that arise from our shared map introduce concepts and ideas that we've never encountered

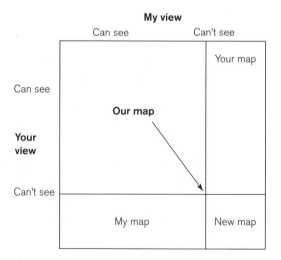

Figure 3.14   *Journey map*

before. The shape and size of the new map quadrant in this matrix is quite deliberate and suggests that there is probably a finite limit to the extent to which you can expand your map by working through the expansion process with one person. The objective is to repeat this exercise with as many people as possible in order to increase and expand the variety of your world view.

Map your map – the three levels

Leader of leaders	**Lead leaders** – Create collective futures that are not restricted by what people believe is difficult – aim to create challenges based on what could be.
Leader of others	**Lead others** – Help others overcome their limiting beliefs and ensure that false fantasies do not permeate the organization.
Leader of self	**Lead yourself** – Be sure that you are not restricting your choices by adopting limiting beliefs. Ensure that you face the facts and don't take on self-generated or other people's fantasies.

Map your map: quick summary

1   Your mental maps are the lenses through which you see and make sense of the world. They are unique to you and are an essential part of who you are and how you lead. If your maps are corrupted they constrain and negate your ability to lead others and yourself.

2 To learn to help others learn you must be able to break up your old maps and create new and more informed views. By breaking and making maps, you effect changes in the way you behave.

3 Your map of the world is not the world; it's a representation of what you choose to observe through biased and subjective lenses. Never accept what you observe as the truth.

4 Positive thinking can help you develop your abilities, but it will be of little use if you're using an out-of-date or inappropriate map of the world.

5 As you reframe messages to fit your maps, don't shift them up the fantasy ladder. By moving an event from fact to fantasy, you're deceiving yourself and, even worse, you might deceive someone else if you pass such a message on.

6 Conflict is caused because your map is different to another's and both of you argue that yours is 'right'.

7 Combining your map with someone else's will create a third map that is richer in variety and experience than the two single maps you started with.

choice four

change how you change

It is only the wisest and the very stupidest
who cannot change.

Confucius

THE ABILITY to manage personal change can be regarded as a new form of security. In the more traditional organization, security is based on the acquisition of power: the power to hold resources, discipline people, control finances and build personal empires. In organizations that value knowledge, people's ability to synthesize the energy of change and learning ultimately offers a greater degree of influence and control than the ability to accumulate hierarchical power, and therefore change offers greater security.

We are in many ways talking about a new form of leadership, namely the transitional leader. For many people each new day brings a different initiative or project that will disrupt the incumbent systems and processes. Each day brings with it the need to manage the transition from one position to another – and manage it with speed, efficiency and confidence.

This need for transitional leadership might be at a personal level; where the constant upsizing and downsizing of corporate dynamics mean that people's life's and careers are endlessly being challenged. Or it might be at a corporate or global level – where ongoing and unexpected world occurrences impact in a critical way on what we might have considered to be a stable point. The relentless rise in terrorism, shifting consumer markets and geopolitical shifts means that corporate markets also shift on an almost daily basis. Hence transitional leadership is the core differentiator for the new brand of leaders. Their ability to deliver swift and appropriate responses to the changes in the marketplace will make a huge difference. The question then is how we create this kind of adaptive response – one where people can manage change in a way that is suitable and not based upon what they normally do.

The process of change can be managed using four styles that vary in structure and visibility. Once you understand the core change you wish to make, think about the style and manner in which you'll manage the transformation. For example, if you want to manage your next career or job move, will you set things out in detail and plan when your change will be and how it will be managed?

There are four basic styles of transitional change:

- **Accidental**. You have a clear understanding of where you want to go, but you don't have a clear process to get there. You're happy to leave events to fate on the basis that the environment is so dynamic that overt control will never work. This might be how you plan a travelling holiday, write a paper at work, decorate the house or design the garden.

- **Backstage**. You have a clear plan of the way that the change will be managed, but much of the action takes place in corridors or shadow areas. The backstage model is one that we use more than we realize, persuading the children to eat their cabbage; hiding a pill in the dog's food; or flirting with the boss's PA to get some time in his diary.

- **Controlled**. You follow a planned and visible structure of change, which means making the assumption that you can predict and control your future according to a set of rules. This might be seen in the way we buy a new house or build a garden shed.

- **Debate**. Here shift happens through the power of dialogue. You're open about the change and talk to people about the transformation, but don't have a structured approach to how it might be delivered. This might be seen in the way you create a team purpose statement at work or agree the menu for a dinner party.

While your natural and preferred change style might have served you well to date, to survive and prosper in a turbulent world you need to have as broad a range of styles in your personal toolkit as possible. If your natural style is control, then the accidental approach offers a strong counterbalance, whereas if your natural preference is the backstage fashion, the ability to use debate might soften what is perceived as a political approach to change. The ability and desire to choose how you change can increase your flexibility and ability to operate in a complex and confusing marketplace.

Change choice

Choosing a change style is determined by the factors that you can influence in the decision-making process. There are two primary choices to be made. First, to what extent will the change be planned? Should every detail be finalized well in advance of the change commencing or can things be left to chance? Second, how visible will the change be? Is it to be controlled and managed openly or will it be hidden from sight?

In considering these two drivers, it's possible to identify the four change styles already set out, namely, accidental, backstage, controlled and debate. By looking in more depth at each of these four styles, we can develop a simple change management matrix (see Figure 4.1). Each of the four quadrants has a particular change style which can be applied in different circumstances.

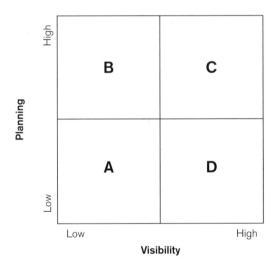

Figure 4.1   *Change choice*

Accidental style

When a group of young children play together where there is
no formal leader to dictate how they play and interact, their
play has an almost chaotic feel. The chance of anything
productive coming out of their antics is accidental in nature.
However, there are a number of powerful rules that control
how the group operates.

The children are effectively operating as a self-organizing
system. Although a parent or teacher has set out a number of
ground rules, for example, no swearing, no playing on the
road, the children are allowed to operate as free agents. Since
the parents or teachers are also aware of these rules, they can
initiate a change and, within reason, guarantee that a desired
outcome is achieved. Just drawing some white lines will
trigger games associated with the patterns. And the children
understand that when the whistle blows, they are expected to
stop and listen for instructions.

Translate this to a work environment. A regional manager in
a retail organization has stock wastage higher then the
industry norm. She must reduce it to an acceptable level. One
option is to issue dictates, discipline people or change the
formal stock control procedures. This might seem to work but
the ingrained behaviours are likely to surface at a later date
once the manager's attention is focused elsewhere. However,
by using the accidental methodology, the manager can
attempt to understand what rules or norms cause the wastage
to happen and why it's seen as acceptable by local managers.
It might be that at the store level, wastage costs are attributed
to a hidden budget line, visible only to the regional manager

and the finance department, so the operational managers are not actually affected by the wastage and it's not part of their frame of reference. By simply changing the bonus indicators, the regional manager might be able to deliver a radical reduction in wastage. The change will have been managed without any real control or planning and its visibility is limited, but the end result is a successful change.

Accidental change is a high-risk strategy and is reliant on the trust of the organization to adopt any changes promoted by the management team. The manager's role is about helping to develop a suitable environment for the change to occur rather than formalizing any direct approach. With this style you must love the turbulence. To lead yourself and others effectively you must be able to adapt to the chaotic forces that surround your life. When taking action that is designed to produce a specific outcome, unexpected responses are to be anticipated and actively welcomed. Therefore the key attribute for any individual who seeks to control their life is to be gloriously happy when working with uncertainty.

Backstage style

Remember the millions of people who went to see the film *Titanic*. The boat scenes are truly amazing, to the point where the audience believes they're actually part of the production. Although star actors play a critical front-stage role, it's often the backstage people that can make or break such a film. The power of the backstage processes is apparent.

The key to managing any backstage process is preparation, preparation and more preparation. Just to get a simple scene in a film will take hours and sometimes days of pre-production effort. The installation of a new IT system, the shift to a new quality directive or the adoption of a new legal ruling – all of these will be highly managed and planned but will in the main be invisible to the end user.

The backstage approach requires your exercise of power, persuasion and political skills. It involves intervening in political and cultural systems, influencing, negotiating, selling ideas and meanings to the owners and recipients of the change and mobilizing the necessary power to effect the backstage activity.

Imagine you're going to install a new quality system into a medium-sized manufacturing company. You might choose to operate across a number of backstage areas. The first step is to agree the content of the system with the company directors. Next, you need to negotiate with the key stakeholders to ensure that the content of the system fits with their map of the world. Finally, much of the backstage work will be focused on managing people's feelings. So, although there will be effort applied in developing the new system, a large chunk of the work will be focused on the backstage issues, the unseen aspects that will never be apparent to the end user.

When the backstage approach is overtly used, you must be careful that you're not seen to be using the process in a duplic-itous way for personal gain.

In working with a client group, there will always be a degree of suspicion about your actions. When this model is used it's imperative that it's used openly and without any hidden agendas. This doesn't mean that you go round telling everyone what's happening, simply that if people ask about the process being used you take time to explain it.

Controlled style

Controlled change is best used when managing large processes, for example, a large construction project like the channel tunnel. The sheer scale and risk means that everything down to the last nut and bolt must be forecast and controlled to ensure that the change is managed to time, cost and quality.

The control model is based on a deterministic framework. This means you assume that it's possible to predict and control the future according to a set of rules. Plans are made, resources booked and people hired on the premise that the change will follow a known path. The change is then managed using the exception method, where the goal is to minimize any variance or disturbance in the system. Accidents will be frowned on, deviation isn't allowed and failure to hit a milestone will cause apoplexy. This method is perfect for the delivery of fixed outcomes, particularly where the plan is built using logical cause-and-effect reasoning. But, with a rigid plan, all your eggs are definitely in one basket.

Debate style

Think about a merger between two large organizations. Project managers, probably using the control method outlined above, will wrap up all the mechanistic issues. However, there will be elements of the merger that can't be managed using a highly planned style. There is likely to be a large amount of debate and dialogue as people struggle to come to terms with new working cultures. Only through a process of sharing and working together will people start to understand what value their new partners will be able to contribute.

The debate style of change is seen in many areas. In reality, corporate strategy emerges from dialogue and debate that goes on between the key players in the business. This might happen in formal meetings but in many cases it takes place through the odd comment as people meet in corridors or coffee rooms.

The debate model happens all the time but is often not recognized, since it's so natural and embedded in the content of the change. The benefit is that when the change takes place, it's locked in at the desired level in the change ladder, which guarantees a greater degree of passion and permanence.

The emergent style

By drawing on all four styles, you can develop a holistic framework, a hybrid model that builds on the strengths of each but avoids their weaknesses (see Figure 4.2).

If a group of people decide to travel around the world on a back-packing holiday, which of the four styles would be appropriate? The accidental approach is exciting but could leave them sitting as hostages in some war zone. The backstage model would be ineffective because only the travel agent would know the itinerary. The control model seems to

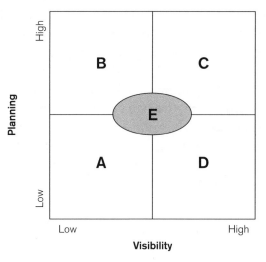

Figure 4.2   *Visibility, planning*

be the most practical, but using a deterministic approach in a chaotic world will only lead to frustration and cost increases as the travellers struggle to keep in line with 'the plan'. Finally the debate model is pretty inappropriate since the group might have fun discussing where to go next but the trip will probably take three years longer than expected. Realistically, there is a need to adopt a change process that produces clearly defined outcomes with necessary flexibility.

In considering the five-segment model, each of the four primary models (accidental, backstage, control and debate) has a clear role to play in managing change. Emergent style is practised widely but not knowingly. Your life is often in tension between planned and unplanned events; it's a battle between order and disorder seen in the deletions and changes in your diary. However, your ability to manage unplanned and emergent interactions allows you to respond to changes in the marketplace. The emergent model gives you the flexibility to adapt and respond to any situation that work or life might throw at you. You have the discipline to tightly manage a problem that has to be delivered within a set timescale; the flexibility to work with a team of people who don't wish to be overtly controlled; the skills to use conversations and dialogue as a way to change how people think and feel; and the shrewdness to operate in the backstage area when a high profile would be detrimental.

Change how you change– the three levels

Leader of leaders	**Lead leaders** – Look over the horizon to assess what market shifts are coming and then help the leaders prepare for any changes that might be necessary.
Leader of others	**Lead others** – Help others understand what their preferred change style is and then learn how to modify it. Become a role model – someone who can adapt their approach as necessary.
Leader of self	**Lead yourself** – Ensure that you are able and willing to adapt and modify your change style as needed.

Change how you change: quick summary

Leadership results in change, and change needs leadership.

1　The journey to effective leadership will always entail some degree of transformation or change. Therefore you need to have different change maps, alternative routes you can take to achieve the desired outcome. Abdication of the choice to manage change is a failure to lead.

2　Any change, whether it's personal or corporate is systemic. It's impossible to change one part of the system without impacting on another in some way. Failure to understand the systemic nature of change leads to persistent failure wherever managed change occurs.

3　The four change styles are accidental, backstage, control and debate. Accidental change offers freedom and creativity but comes with the risk of non-completion where the outcome is unclear. Backstage change offers huge returns as the political and social systems are managed but it can appear selfish or clandestine. Control change can deliver in mission-critical situations but may limit the spirit and resourcefulness of the people involved. Debate change opens up the change process for all to get involved but can lead to chaos as the people take over – the optimum position is to adopt an emergent style where you have the freedom and flexibility to use any of the four styles at any moment.

05

choice five

step inside out

Until you walk a mile in another man's moccasins
you can't imagine the smell.

Robert Byrne

AT SOME stage you'll need to work and collaborate with others to create a shared success. The core driver to achieve this rests in your ability to 'step inside out' – effectively to walk in their shoes and truly understand what is important for others before you seek to tell them what is important for you.

The core of this ability rests on your willingness and ability truly to understand the other person and the maps they use to make sense of the world. Importantly, this really is about understanding other people, and not just finding the latest technique for getting along better with them. By seeking to understand them and their maps we are beginning truly to understand what's important to them.

If you are trying to create a successful relationship with one of today's teenagers, it's not going to do much good to take them to see one of the dinosaur bands from the 1970s. Instead, you must try to look at them carefully enough to see what's important to them – and so make what's important to them become important to you. This willingness to understand and enquire about the other person's maps will help to create an unselfish, shared success. This offers the sharing of a collaborative outcome where all the players are happy with the end result. But before you can define a good end result you must know what meaning another person applies to the outcome and how they determine what shared success looks like. To do this you must step out of your universe and into theirs.

The 'step inside out' choice covers the following ideas:

- **Thick Trust**. With relationships grounded in trust, the relationship will be open, transferable and often celebrated. Where a relationship is grounded in distrust, power bases and back-biting, success will be token, short-lived and sour.

- **Multiverse management**. We often make decisions based on the idea of a universe where our view of the world is the right view. But our world view is just one that exists in a 'multiverse', a multitude of alternative intersecting universes where an infinite number of differing versions of reality exist and interact.

- **Three-step reframe**. This is a technique where you can step outside your view of the world and get second and third perspectives of a relationship so that you're better able to enhance how the relationship operates and as a result achieve sustainable, shared success.

Creating thick trust

Trust is the fulcrum that can effect different degrees of leverage in a relationship. By shifting the fulcrum towards the high-trust direction, you can quantify the reduction in time taken to solve problems and work effectively. Within an organization the transaction costs reduce if less money is spent on monitoring and control processes. If people don't have to worry about making mistakes and protecting their turf, they're more willing to open up and share learning and knowledge. Correspondingly, as the fulcrum shifts the other way, trust diminishes, power battles erupt, tribal camps form and the flow of knowledge is attenuated.

However, trust isn't a simple switch that can be turned on and off at will. The giving and taking of trust can vary considerably in its fragility and resilience, and can change quickly or slowly depending on the circumstances. Trust associated with a close personal friendship is resilient and durable, and can be regarded as thick trust. Once established, it's not easily disrupted, but once shattered, it isn't readily repaired or restored. In casual or short-term relationships, we see thin trust. This is the type conferred on a project group or product team, where people only tend to commit part of themselves.

Trust funds

It took me a long time to realize that I can't really achieve anything successful in my life without the help of others. Delivering something in life that has value and is sustainable can only be achieved by working in partnership with others, people who have a shared goal and will work towards the same or shared outcome.

How do you build and maintain such productive relationships? What are the critical factors that you put in place both to identify people you can work with and to maintain the relationships over a satisfactory time? They are all centred on the notion of trust.

Think about a manager who has a team of ten people. If the manager doesn't really trust a number of people in the team, a large percentage of that manager's personal time is spent on low-value activities – putting control systems in place, running audits and checking all the work flows and outputs. Conversely, where a manager has a trust-based relationship with all members of the team, the vast majority of the manager's time will be spent adding value and developing the capabilities of the team members.

No real surprise there. This is a common theme, but how do you learn to develop and manage trust in order to actively manage relationships?

The problem with trust is that it's like a good partnership – you know it when you see it, but it's hard to define the individual contributing factors. As an example, think about someone who you know well and trust implicitly. What is it that makes you think of that person? What do they and you do to maintain the relationship? Now think of another person you know just as well but don't trust. Consider what it is that each of you does to create a relationship lacking in substance and value. What's the impact of such a relationship and what overheads does it impose? If you ask them to do a job or help you out, to what extent do you have to give up valuable personal time to check and oversee the work? Do you lose sleep because there is a fear in the back of your mind that they might not deliver on time or to standard?

In many ways, the time you spend building relationships with others is an investment process, where you choose to offer and invest your personal time and capital. If you end up spending a large portion of your time with people who actually turn out to be untrustworthy, it feels awful. Do you have relationships where this might happen? Just think, would you take a big chunk of your wages each month and place it into an account that only promised to waste your money with the result that your return is less than your investment. For me, the abuse of my personal time is as big a waste as losing money and is something I consciously guard against. Relationships are like saving accounts – we put time and energy into them in the hope that the shared success will grow and multiply, in the same way that investments in a trust fund will produce compound growth over time. Measuring your relationships might seem artificial but, like your finances, you should be aware of the amounts that you've invested in different places, monitor the levels of performance each supplier is offering and where necessary make changes to improve the return.

Managing your investment

I have a simple definition of trust that I use to measure and manage relationships:

- **Truthful** – the extent to which integrity, honesty and truthfulness are developed and maintained.

- **Responsive** – the openness, mental accessibility or willingness to share ideas and information freely.

- **Uniform** – the degree of consistency, reliability and predictability contained within the relationship.

- **Safe** – the loyalty, benevolence or willingness to protect, support and encourage each other.

- **Trained** – the competence, technical knowledge and capabilities of both parties.

Where these five attributes are soundly in place, the nature of the relationship might have the characteristics of a thick-trust interaction. Conversely, where one or more of the factors is diminished or missing, it's possible the relationship is suffering from thin trust.

Leaders invest in people as well as banks

To what extent do you manage the trust levels with people you work with and care for?

In the same way that you have credits and debits with your bank, you also have a trust fund with all the people you interact with where debits and credits are applied on a daily basis.

I've seen this so clearly with my daughter Lucy as she has grown up. When Lucy first started school she found a best friend and they were sure that the relationship would stay that way for the rest of their lives – until one day this friend talked about her behind her back or told a small lie. The first time this happened they had an argument and made up. The second time it happened the relationship became strained and

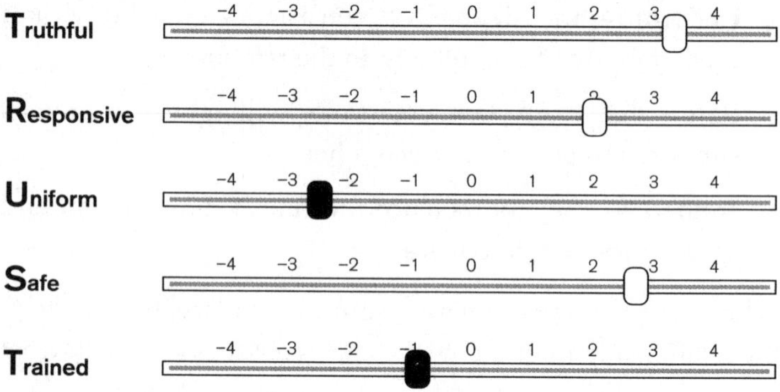

Figure 5.1   *Trust*

the third time they wandered off to find new best friends for life. The split occurred because Lucy's friend took so many withdrawals from the trust fund that it fell below the level needed to sustain a relationship.

For any relationship it's very easy for us to move the account sliders on the account into credit or debit (see Figure 5.1). When I run a training session I only have to tell a lie about something to weaken the truthful slider; ignore a question by someone for them to feel that I'm not being responsive; tell two people different things to upset the uniform balance; tell a story about someone else to raise concerns about how safe people feel; or appear not to be a competent trainer to reduce the value in the trained sub-account. Slippage in any one area of the trust fund erodes my personal value and even worse reduces my chance to create a shared success with the delegates on the course.

Your high is my hurt

Making deposits and withdrawing credits on your trust fund is not as easy as you might think. Just do someone a favour and you're in credit or upset them and you're in debit? Life isn't quite that simple. A while ago I managed to get some tickets to watch a key England *v.* Germany match on television at our local bar (tickets were sold because of the enormous demand). I thought my sons Matt and Michael would enjoy it. As a great football fan, Matt was really delighted. Michael also came with us but after a while he looked uncomfortable. It turned out that he didn't really like that particular bar and would have preferred not to be there after all. In my enthusiasm to watch the match with the boys I failed to be responsive to Michael's individual needs, and what I thought was a credit turned out to be a debit. Where trust funds are concerned it's crucial to understand that a credit is a credit in the eye of the receiver, not the giver.

As a further example, I used to work for a firm who were keen to praise and reward people who produced quality work and at the end of the year they organized a quality award event (where people get called up on to the podium to receive a round of applause and a certificate). When I was given the honour of receiving one of these awards, I was actually mortified about parading in front of 300 people to receive it. My manager's trust fund deposit was, for me, not quite the credit he had envisaged.

Think about how you currently reward people who help you out or perform well. To what extent are you giving them credits that might be perceived as debits? Do you take people out for a beer to celebrate even if they are introverts, or do you talk to them privately when maybe they want it to be shouted from the heavens? The challenge is to think about the credit/debit relationship, and if you really want to make a deposit in someone's trust fund, make sure you understand their map, don't impose your own.

Transferable trust

By managing trust, your trust fund becomes attractive to other people with a result that your account can be transferred in real time. Think about the last time you sat round a dinner table with a group of friends or went for a drink with some work colleagues. Inevitably, group conversation turns to people's opinions of absent colleagues or friends. I guarantee that if you hear two or more people describe their experience of the same person in positive terms, their trust account will look attractive and you'll be more prepared to make an investment if you happen to meet that person.

We recently had to employ a builder to carry out some work in the house. I've been caught before by cowboy builders who come in, mess about for a while, slap up some paint and then charge the earth for a poor job that will only last a short while. So this time I decided to talk with the people who own the local hardware store. I trusted them and believed that anyone they suggested would be reliable. In this sense the trust fund they have with the builder was transferred to me – the builders' trust account was already in credit when they arrived (see Figure 5.2).

	−4	−3	−2	−1	0	1	2	3	4
Truthful									

	−4	−3	−2	−1	0	1	2	3	4
Responsive									

	−4	−3	−2	−1	0	1	2	3	4
Uniform									

	−4	−3	−2	−1	0	1	2	3	4
Safe									

	−4	−3	−2	−1	0	1	2	3	4
Trained									

Figure 5.2 *Trust*

Once they started work the account sliders went into even more credit. Within five minutes I could tell that they were trained; I believed that they were telling me the truth and I felt safe enough to leave them alone in the house. The end result was that we achieved a shared success. They've been well paid for their work and I got my new wall with a minimum of fuss and inconvenience; and the trust transfer continues when I recommend them to friends. Without a positive trust fund the whole relationship would collapse and opportunities to share success would be shattered.

Once the thick trust has been attained you can start to effect a relationship that is both shared and sustainable.

Multiverse management

The effective leader is able to present and frame the outcomes they need to achieve in a language and style that makes sense to the recipients. Clearly, trying to encourage a 4-year-old child to keep their bedroom tidy because of the health implications might not make much sense but framing it in such a way that they understand they'll be able to make space for even more toys and have friends to sleep over might make better sense.

If you see someone behaving in a way that you view as wrong or unacceptable, you have to remember that their behaviour is working for them, and once you see why it works for them and what value they get from it, you'll understand it; then you can start to accept it and feel differently about it. To achieve this type of reframe in the way you think, feel and behave, you need to step inside out: your inner self steps out of you, and into the person with whom you wish to share success.

Let go of some of your preconceptions, assumptions and biases and start to understand what internal drivers cause other people to behave in a certain way. For example, you might know of someone whom you would describe as overbearing, directive and dictatorial. How do you react when you are with them? Is your behaviour defensive, aggressive, submissive? If you were to step inside (let's call him) Jim's body and experience, the pains and problems he faces every day, you would start to appreciate just why he appears to be such a control freak. Perhaps he lost his last job because he gave people in the team freedom to behave responsibly and with integrity, and the team abused his trust, which led to lost business and resulted in Jim's dismissal. Maybe the personal consequences of Jim's dismissal were even greater; having lost his accompanying medical benefits, his wife was moved from a private hospital to a public hospital 100 miles away from the family. As a consequence he's not prepared to be in a situation again where he offers trust to employees until he's absolutely sure that it won't put his career and family life in jeopardy. By making this leap, you start to understand what is driving others' behaviour and you can develop the right approach to bridge these problems and demonstrate that the other person can trust you.

The notion of a multiverse is crucial in any step-inside-out decision. Standing on your side of the fence you can never see someone else's problem. The first stage in understanding someone else's world view is simply acknowledging that their world exists and is related to but different from yours. You can then move on to walking in their shoes and seeing the world as they see it. First, however, you have to reframe your

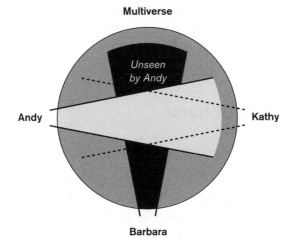

Figure 5.3 *Multiverse*

world orientation – that means taking a multidimensional view.

Reframing your world view allows you access to different perspectives and how they are formed. Reframing is an essential tool in conflict resolution and relationship management.

In Figure 5.3 Andy has a problem with one of his team members, Barbara. No matter how much he tries he can't seem to resolve it. He sees that her performance is down and his efforts to help don't work. But he has failed to see this from Barbara's perspective. As a single person with no commitments, Andy is driven by work, money and fun. As a single mother Barbara is driven by her family, work and rest. Unless Andy is able to step into her shoes, walk her walk and experience her life then it doesn't matter how much encouragement or extra financial inducement he offers her to improve, nothing will work. By thinking, feeling and acting as she does, he will be able to understand what factors will help to generate shared success.

Three-step reframe

There are times when this book does not make sense.

Maybe you agree? Or perhaps you strongly disagree. Someone flicking through this book in the bookshop will see that statement and think 'I'm not buying that book', but someone else will choose to buy it because they're encouraged by the fact that I put such a statement in my own book. The statement, which is common to us all, produces different thoughts, feelings and behaviours because we're all using different frames. By learning to change the frame you use to make sense of the world, you can change the meaning; and when the meaning changes for you, changes in your behaviour will follow suit.

Have you ever baby-sat for someone in their house? You have to reorient yourself to a whole new set of rules. Things that you see as truths are no longer necessarily correct; in many cases, they're completely wrong. But you have to follow the other person's rules. For example, you might have brought your children up on one type of medicine but another parent might ask you to use a different type for their child. Following someone else's rules can make you feel awkward, uncomfortable and uneasy.

Now think of three people you know well but who don't have similar lifestyles to yours. Be honest, to what extent could you reframe into their life and describe their universe? Could you describe what they think and worry about each day, what problems they face, or what they do each day to earn a living?

The three-step reframe technique will help you tap into others' world views in order to answer these questions, and to move forward together to generate shared success.

The first stage of the three-step reframe is to consider the relationship from three different perspectives: yours; the other person's; and a stranger's. The second stage is to view the relationship from different perspectives using the heart, head and hand dimensions. These two shifts are called position and dimension step reframes. Combining them into a single model allows you to draw out a detailed picture of your relationship with someone else.

Position steps

In the position reframe, you rotate round a relationship to gather new perspectives.

Choose a relationship and move round it taking snapshots from different angles. The first stage is to understand how the relationship looks from your perspective; then from the other person's point of view; and then from a third position where you take a snapshot in the role of detached observer (see Figure 5.4).

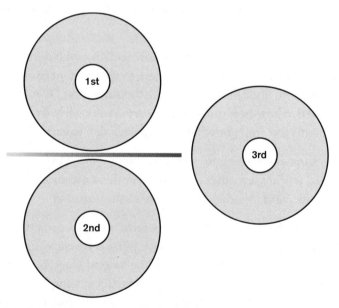

Figure 5.4   *First, second and third positions*

- **Position 1**. Explore the relationship from your position. Look inwards and understand the current maps that you use to make sense of the world and build your universe. Understand how you view your relationship with the other person; what is happening within the relationship from your perspective and what you're doing to manage the relationship. Although in theory you'd expect to know much of this already, sometimes it can help to just sit back and ask yourself, how do I feel about this person or situation? Once you have a clear understanding of your own view of the relationship with the other person, then consciously move to the second step.

- **Position 2**. Move into the other person's role. Make a conscious effort to understand their universe. Try to see their problems, feel their pain, understand what daily issues they face and importantly understand how they regard the relationship with you. You should begin a shift from your universe to the other person's. You can start to get new information about the relationship. You might start to understand that what you see as supportive is perceived by others as smothering, or relaxed to you might be sloppy to them. Now, you've started to step inside out and to view a world that exists outside your own.

- **Position 3**. Finally, step into the role of the independent observer or dissociated commentator, who stands back from the relationship and considers what's going on between these two people. How well do they work together? What are the elements that are less effective? I've often seen this position used by directors in companies to test their strategies. Their acid test is: how would the newspapers view the strategy? A laboured and tortuous strategy development process could be seen as a positive plan, or it might be rubbished as a failed intervention. The decision to accept or reject the strategy isn't necessarily made on the basis of such a question, but the third position acts as a safety gate to ensure that silly mistakes aren't made.

Once you've considered your relationships from all three perspectives, move back to the first position. Back at home, you can start to make decisions on what action is needed based on your new frame.

Imagine the three-step frame in action; for instance, use it to improve the relationship with your manager. At position one, your perception is that you're not allowed any slack. Your manager doesn't give you space to take a few risks or make a name for yourself. In position two, you start to understand that what you see as her failure to let go of the reins is influenced by your failure to submit paperwork on time. In position three, step back and recognize the problem: it's less about personalities and more about management styles. You prefer to operate in a relaxed and spontaneous way; your field experience has taught you to focus on getting the job done, and paperwork comes last. Your manager prefers a structured approach; her finance background means she understands just how important it is to manage the flow of paperwork so that billing takes place on time. With all this data, step back into position one and consider what action you can take to achieve a more collaborative approach.

Dimension steps

By incorporating the head, heart and hand dimension in the process, the step-inside-out process becomes richer. At each of the three steps, try to get information on the thoughts, feelings and behaviours in these positions (see Figure 5.5).

Heart steps, for example, say you want to enhance your relationship with your partner. You've had a few arguments lately and you want to understand the problem and how to resolve it. From the first position, look at why you're behaving the way you do, where the relationship is at the moment and where you believe it's heading. From a heart perspective, try and understand why you choose to feel the way you do; consider why you choose the particular responses you make to your partner's comments.

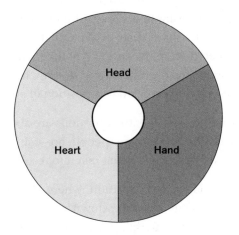

Figure 5.5   *Head, heart, hand*

Heart questions focus on why someone is doing something and where the relationship is heading.

Move to the second position. The heart questions can be asked again. Why does your partner choose to get into the fight? Why do they respond to verbal challenges in the way they do? What do they hope to achieve from the argument? What future do they see in the relationship? Their emotional goals and drivers might be very different from yours. Ideally, at this point you should be developing an understanding of what differences exist at deep emotional levels between you and in what ways you view the future differently. The important thing here is not to focus on the arguments but to understand how each of you makes sense of your own universe.

In the third position, imagine yourself sitting in a cinema watching a film of these two people fighting. Why are they arguing? Are their arguments about a real issue, or are they a symptom of their desire to achieve different life goals? Have they taken time to share their goals and desires with each other or are they held in darkness? Are they willing to make real choices about the argument, and do they have the inner security to resolve the problem in a position of strength?

Using the head perspective, the questions are about defining and understanding what maps people are using, how they differ and what approach is being taken to resolve problems.

Imagine that you're in a position where the relationship with your manager is breaking down. Over recent months you've been arguing, niggling each other and generally failing to agree on the way that problems might be resolved. You have decided that the position is untenable, both for you and the other members of the team, who have to deal with the fallout.

In the first position you need to understand your own map. Consider how you see the current situation, what you find acceptable and unacceptable. Have you climbed the fantasy ladder? What are the real facts? Use any of the topics covered in the map-your-map section to gain clarity over how you view the situation.

Understanding the other person's map is the objective in the second position. What degree of variety do they have in the way they look at things? What do they view as acceptable and unacceptable? What is their standard operating procedure? Do they view you as an individual or as just another member of their team? And what shadow maps are operating? In essence, how do they make sense of the world and how do they view their relationship with you?

Finally, view the situation from a detached position. If you were to read a similar story in the newspaper, who would you say is to blame? Where do the two people share similar ideas and where do they differ? To what extent is there a way of thinking that will satisfy both their needs? Once you've commented on the relationship from the third position, step back to the first position and respond to your advice.

In hand reframe you try to experience the physical environment of the other person. A hand reframe for a managing director might be to work with the customer service people for a while to understand the problems they have when dealing with irate customers. Or, a member of the customer service team could spend a day covering the manager's position to get a feel for the problems of senior management.

I had a much less glamorous experience one week when I stepped out of my usual frame and helped my sons with their paper round, which they had been doing for a couple of years. Every Wednesday the papers would be delivered to our house and they would insert advertising leaflets ready for delivery on Thursday. I had some free time so I thought I would help them out. Unfortunately, the week I chose to help was cold, raining and blowing up a real gale. I told them my stories of when I used to be a paperboy and go out in 'weather that was ten times worse than this!'. I thought I knew it all. But I soon ate my words. I couldn't believe how many houses had small yappy dogs whose only passion in life is to attack your fingertips when you push the paper through, and they're ably helped by modern-day post flaps whose large coil springs have enough torque to raise the *Titanic*. It takes Herculean strength just to open the flap, and then once your fingers are in they jam shut just above the knuckles so the dog can get them. The papers weigh a ton and the gardens have all sorts of lethal obstacles – broken gates, wonky paving and thorny bushes. With my souvenirs of the day – a twisted ankle, sore fingers and damaged pride – I realized I'd far sooner face a baying crowd of angry executives than have a paper round these days. Sometimes we really have to get our hands dirty and physically experience what others go through in order to understand their part in a relationship.

Three-step reframe: position and dimension

The real power of reframing using the different dimensions comes when you're able to step into each position and consider it with all three dimensions (see Figure 5.6). With any problem which you wish to resolve in a relationship, look at it from all angles. Use the following sets of questions as a guide:

In the first position, consider:

- How do I feel about this relationship?
- Where do I believe it's heading?
- What do I think is right and wrong with it?

How have I tried to resolve the problem, for example, with subtlety, spontaneity or in an open and planned way?

In the second position:

- How do I feel about the other person (me, that is)?
- How are we behaving towards each other?
- Why do I think this is happening?
- How would I like the other person to behave?
- How would I feel if they changed?
- What would I do in response?

In the third position (the independent view), ask:

- How are these people behaving towards each other?
- How do I feel about their behaviour?
- Is either of them in the wrong?

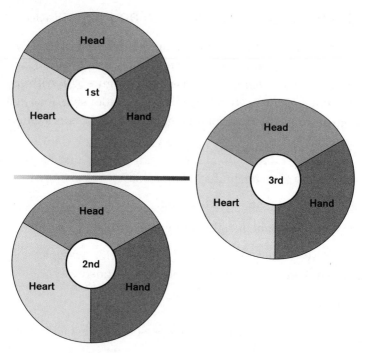

Figure 5.6 *Three positions*

- Why do I think this is happening?
- What advice would I give to the first person to help them improve the relationship?

Once you've completed the three-step reframe process, reflect on the insights that the other positions have offered and try to effect a real solution that will enhance the relationship.

Step barriers

The theory seems quite simple: just put yourself in the other person's shoes and all is well. Not quite. People like being where they are and don't like to move to positions that are unnatural for them. If you ask them to step into the role of someone they don't get along with or don't like, the barriers really come up and in many cases people simply refuse. It's this refusal and unwillingness to see the world from another person's perspective that leads to problems in the first place.

If you are to operate on the principle of shared success, then a number of logical, physical and emotional blockages need to be managed and overcome so that you are able to see another person's point of view.

- **Legacy experiences**. Our past experiences can distort our view. We have a video recorder in our head that has a stock-pile of film clips that can instantly replay that bad or embarrassing moment we had with someone years ago. So you need to develop the ability to archive the film clips. You don't have to erase past incidents, just learn to put them to one side while you try to live in their universe.

- **Bias**. Communication between people is frequently distorted when one person decides in advance that the other isn't worth listening to. Imagine the West Ham footballer who's asked to understand the universe a Tottenham supporter lives in. The instant response is 'No way'. Years of conditioning and bias kick in and a barrier to the step-inside-out process is erected. This can be seen at work all the time as tribal walls are established between functional or regional groups. The northerners hate the southerners, and vice versa; the engineers hate the sales reps. If you are to manage the step-inside-out process, you must catch this bias and put it in temporary storage before it blocks your ability to effect a change.

- **Status**. Perhaps the most difficult barrier to overcome in making the shift is status. Any difference in status power, authority or position can make the shift difficult. It can be hard to understand how someone else acquires and employs their power base. Do they use the status as a foil to drive and effect change in an open and discussable way, or is it a shadow factor, where their power is inferred and managed as a backstage operation?

Enabling strategies

However, there are certain simple strategies that can be employed to enable the process.

- **No one makes a bad decision**. This is possibly the most difficult mental switch to make. Think about the statement, 'no one makes a bad decision'. Everyone, whoever they are, makes the best possible decision that they can at any particular moment in time. This is the colleague who decided to usurp your authority and set up a programme office in a different location, or the teenager who decided to take drugs. To you, they might be decisions that you don't agree with, but at the instant the decision was made it was the right one for them. Based on all the data, resourses and evidence, they made a choice. They might regret it later, but at that moment it was their best possible decision. If you can't accept this principle, you'll be entering someone else's universe through a critical frame rather than an enquiring one and blockages will exist from the outset.

- **Live the context**. Wherever possible, try to adopt the second position in the environment the other person operates in. If you're a managing director who wants to develop an appreciation of problems at the coalface, you could think yourself into the role of engineer or sales agent, but it's unlikely that you'll appreciate the detail of the problems they face on a daily basis without stepping into the context in which they work.

- **Manage the inner voice**. One of the difficulties with stepping into a secondary or third position is that your inner voice still has a say over how you think, feel and behave. In an ideal world you would close the inner voice down and focus on the voice of the person whose shoes you're walking in. However, the reality is that it takes an amazing amount of will power and personal control to shut down this internal stream of thoughts. One of the ways to overcome this is not to try to close the voice down, but just to accept that the inner voice is challenging the second and third position thoughts; have a dialogue with it from these positions. What you're doing is taking a viewpoint different from your own and reinforcing your transition to your new position by arguing with yourself.

- **Go third first**. Imagine you want to build a relationship with someone at work who you find really irritating. You might understand the need to step inside out but the thought of taking their view of the world feels absolutely appalling. Try jumping straight into the third position.

Look at the relationship from a detached position. Once you've stepped into the relatively safe, objective position it then becomes much easier to move to the second position.

- **Separate the relationship from the person**. When in the second position, try to think about the individual in whose shoes you're walking; don't initially focus on how they feel about their relationship with you. The essence of the step-inside-out choice is to understand the person first, then, once you understand the individual's drivers, their relationship with you. If you immediately focus on how they interact with you, it makes it more difficult to separate yourself.

These techniques may help, but to really find the most effective way for you to step to the second and third positions, you'll need to practise, and in doing so develop your own strategies and styles.

Step inside out – the three levels

Leader of leaders	**Lead leaders** – Always seek to understand the dreams and wishes of the leadership team. By virtue of the fact that people lead they will often have high motivational and entrepreneurial needs. As such the meta leader needs to be constantly in touch with this and learn how to optimize the positive aspect and also counter any potentially destructive outcomes that such drive and power can trigger across the leadership team.
Leader of others	**Lead others** – Always seeks to understand other people's viewpoints before imposing their own. Recognize that their view is not always the right one as other people might be closer to the ground and understand what is going on.
Leader of self	**Lead yourself** – To effectively deliver personal, sustainable success, you need to build bridges with others. To do this you must be able and willing to share what you are thinking and feeling and share your whole self.

Step inside out: quick summary

1   It's very difficult to step inside out and see the world from someone else's perspective. You like being where you are and don't like to move to an unnatural position. But your inability or unwillingness to see the world from

the other person's position reduces the chances of sharing success.

2   You often make decisions based on the idea of a single universe: your own. You have to accept that your world view isn't the only one and that other people's views are equally valid. Your universe is just one with countless others that form a multiverse.

3   No one makes a bad decision or does the wrong thing. If you see someone behaving in a way that you think is wrong or unacceptable you have to accept that the behaviour they've chosen works for them.

4   Behaviour changes with context and will have a totally different meaning, value and outcome. As a leader, your role is to appreciate the many different meanings you can apply to what people do, think and feel.

5   Effective leaders always present ideas and outcomes in a style that makes sense to others.

6   To overcome the fantasy gap created by different legacy and value systems, you must be able to step inside the other person's shoes and understand their maps using the three-step reframe.

7   The three-step reframe requires two changes. First, shift yourself into another person's universe and see life from their perspective. Second, understand the other person's viewpoint via the heart, head and hand dimensions.

share success

Coming together is the beginning.
Keeping together is progress.
Working together is success.

Henry Ford

AS YOU reach a position where you have control over the first five choices in the personal leadership framework, you might find that there's a fine line between being self-confident and being selfish. By having control over your life, you might appear to ignore or override other people's needs. Using your personal power solely to achieve the things you desire will undo the benefits accrued so far. Personal leadership that is selfish and short-lived is not true success. The only real form of personal leadership is one founded on the notion of shared and sustainable outcomes and the key to this choice is the absolute focus on mutual benefit.

Shared success is about using the following tools:

- advocacy and enquiry – the ability to tell others what we expect of them and ask them what they expect of us

- thinking 'compound' – the idea that good begets great, and great begets excellent

- the values bridge – the alignment of our values, our personal value and feeling valued.

Advocacy and enquiry

You can only achieve shared success if you understand what success means for you and others. I see people working together to achieve a shared outcome but they don't really understand what the other person wants to achieve. The end result teeters between a battle of wills as each person struggles to assert their view of success, or lacklustre output because no one has really said what is important for them. If we assume that everyone is different and has distinct goals and ambitions, then we can understand what real success is for the people we work and live with.

Well, it worked for me, so it must work for you!

I've worked in many teams that had larger than life, extrovert managers who, when they come to reward the people in the team, follow a reward pattern that aligns with their view of the world. This might be to take people down to the pub for a big party, put the person's name in banners around the room or publish their success in the company newsletter. This is fine if you're someone who shares those extrovert preferences, but if you're anything like me, more of an introvert, this type of reward is unsettling; I've found it actually reduced my desire to improve on the results next time round. Though with the best of intentions, the manager believes they are sharing their success, in fact they're operating on the basis of a selfish success principle.

However, it isn't the manager's fault if the rewards they think people will value are based on their own preferences. As individuals, we have a say in the matter and a responsibility to be courageous, if that's what it takes, to tell them our preferences and how we'd like to be rewarded. The only way to share success is to operate a push–pull system. A push strategy ensures that others will understand what success means to you, and a pull strategy means you can take time out to understand what success will be for them:

- advocacy – making sure other people know what you want and need by having the courage to tell them

- enquiry – understanding other people's goals, dreams and desires, by showing consideration and seeking to understand what success means for them.

Once you understand these two dimensions you can appreciate how they interrelate and what the consequences are when they are observed in a relationship.

As these two dimensions interact we can realize four different types of success (see Figure 6.1):

- **Selfish**. This is high advocacy and is an appropriate strategy when you have to fight a raging fire. I see this in senior managers who have to rescue a company that has a problem but don't have time to negotiate solutions – they have to set a direction and head for it fast. However, once in this position, you risk not being able to step into a different segment.

- **Squandered**. The result of low advocacy and enquiry skills. You'll see this in committee meetings where people just turn up because the diary says there's a meeting – it means the companies' resources, including its managers' time, are squandered.

● **Subordinate**. This is where you've spent too much time enquiring what success will be for someone else and too little time on what you want out of the relationship. As a parent, you often find yourself seeing to everyone else's needs and subordinating your own; it generally isn't the most productive thing to do as you're spreading your time and talents too thinly, and in the end, no one benefits fully from your efforts, especially you.

● **Shared**. Achieving a balance between: strength and courage to set out just what's important for you, and enough consideration and care to listen to others. This

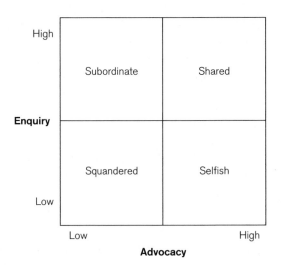

Figure 6.1 *Advocacy, enquiry*

requires genuine listening, not just polite nods and smiles. Unless you're engaged and listening with your heart and your head, you'll never understand what success really means for the people you're with.

Think 'compound'

Success has a wide bandwidth of possibilities. The resolution of a political debate in Parliament is usually viewed as a success. But is this true when the solution is a fudge to get it through the legislative and political process? And does this really draw upon the politician's capabilities to enhance the lives of their constituents? The final bill might simply be a political compromise that satisfies the base needs of each party but doesn't really help transform or resolve some of the deeper problems that weaken society. What's missing is a sense of collaboration and synergistic thinking that takes people's deeper ideas and beliefs and transforms them into something new and original.

Yet another fight in the studio!

Every time I record a new CD, there is some form of negotiation and trade-off between the members of the band. Whose songs do we record? Who takes the solo break? Who sings? And so on. The whole experience is one long stream of negotiated debate that can and often does turn into argument (physical fights are reserved for the more glamorous bands!). Yet our whole objective during the recording and production processes is to avoid compromise and make do. Our goal is to ensure that the relationship operates at a compound level because the true worth of a relationship comes from the ability to create something from nothing. Like investing a pound in a high deposit account and watching it grow effortlessly, investment in compound relationships gives a good return.

This is a really important part of the shared-success quadrant (see Figure 6.2). So often people invest in relationships that process nothing more than the sum of the parts. If you choose to spend time with someone on a project, you're giving away valuable time, energy and ideas. You can't afford to give such resources away if the relationship is going to operate at a level of compromise. Instead, you want to work with people who take your ideas and build on them and whose ideas you can build on in turn. The net result is a compound or synergistic relationship, where the sum of the parts is greater than the whole.

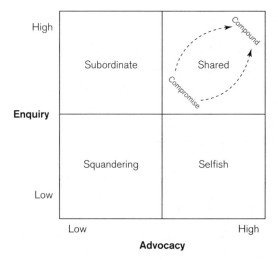

Figure 6.2   *Advocacy, enquiry*

This is such a simple idea but one that people often fail to think about. Most people wouldn't even consider investing their hard earned money in a savings account where the end of year return was the same amount of money. When we invest our personal cash we trust the bank to invest the money wisely in the market and to return interest on a compound basis.

Compound success is founded on two principles. Exposed advocacy, where you're prepared to expose your deep personal success criteria and share them with other people; and empathic enquiry where your goal is to use an enquiry structure that enables the other person to expose their inner personal success criteria. Where both principles are employed a shift is made from compromise to compound success (see Figure 6.3).

Exposed advocacy

Advocacy is about putting forth a personal idea or feeling in order to stimulate a specific outcome. In his book *The Fifth Discipline*, Peter Senge suggests that advocacy is the ability to solve problems by enlisting support, winning arguments and getting things done. It is a head-based process where you present data or logical thought. The head dimension is employed to filter data in and out of the positioning argument in order to ensure that a win is achieved. However, exposed advocacy is a process where you attempt to expose your deep feelings and values to other people to help realize an outcome that satisfies a deeper set of ambitions and needs. The idea is to retain the head function but to achieve a sustained shared success based on shared values, principles and deep desires.

To manage the process of exposed advocacy you must:

- **Expose private wins**. Have a clear and focused understanding of what good means to you. How would you define success from your perspective and how can you make it clear enough for others to understand?

- **Discuss undiscussables**. The essence of exposed advocacy is to bring to the surface the shadow desires, to feel comfortable enough to expose and explain the deep personal factors that really drive your behaviour to another person.

- **Welcome debate**. Offer the recipients the chance to explore and understand the ideas being put forward. Unless the other person feels able to explore the success factors you're aiming for, there is a chance they won't fully understand what the aims are and how they can be achieved.

So that shared success does not fall into selfish success where your effort is one-sided with your needs taking pole position, exposed advocacy should be balanced by empathic enquiry.

Empathic enquiry

You probably think you're a good listener. But how good are you at empathic listening, where the skill is to enquire about the other's person goals by helping to make the unconscious conscious? Enquiry is a formal process to take in information, whereas empathic listening is about listening with the heart without the need to impose your personal interpretations.

Empathic enquiry means you must:

- **Decide to listen**. This might sound silly, but it's the conscious desire to put the tacit receptors into gear and to listen with your heart. This is a very specific and conscious process, not something that simply happens as you're walking along the corridor chatting with someone.

- **Minimize internal distractions**. Develop a sense of rapport and put your own needs, thoughts and values temporarily aside. As we listen to other people describe their goals it's easy for the inner voice to jump in and challenge or disagree with the statement being made. Your inner voice must be tightly managed to ensure it doesn't corrupt the influx of thoughts and feelings from the other person.

- **Love paradox**. You must be able to agree with the speaker's wish to achieve a set of goals, even if you don't agree with the actual goals. This is the art of listening without prejudice and accepting other people's wishes without acting as critic.

- **Clarify on line**. As you manage the enquiry process, you will stimulate a flow of thoughts and feelings from the other person. While this data is flowing inwards you must be able to reflect back and check for understanding.

- **Manage air space**. You must stay conscious of the balance between listening and telling as there is always competition for air space. Try to ensure that the balance is appropriate for the outcome you wish to achieve.

If you can reach a stage where both players in a relationship are able to offer both empathic enquiry and exposed advocacy, you have a genuine and successful relationship. This is where generative learning is being used to help people genuinely understand what shared success might look like and agree how to realize compound shared success.

Imagine you manage a small team of customer service operators in a busy call centre. You've managed the team for the past two years and have a good working relationship with all the members. Two weeks ago Pete, a new member, transferred from a different office to join the team. All went well in the first few days, but at the end of the first week tension emerged. Pete wanted to set up a small project team to review the office procedures, but you felt there was little need for this as the team was functioning well already. You eventually agreed a middle ground. Pete would undertake a personal review of the procedures but not take up the valuable time of any of the other team members.

However, a few days later, Pete published his findings without your agreement. The result was that the divisional manager became involved and started to question why changes were being proposed to the procedures without her agreement. You face a dilemma: should you take Pete to one side and really lay down the law as to the expected behaviours within the team; or should you try to understand what deeper issues were being played out in the team? Using the idea of empathic enquiry and exposed advocacy, you arrange to spend some time with Pete to try and agree how you can best work together. Rather than telling Pete how he should approach his job, you try to understand why he took the action he did and what he'd hoped to achieve by running the project.

After a while it turns out that Pete is paying to put himself through a degree school at evening class. He's spent many years at the same level in the organization, but has decided to seek promotion and he sees the move to your team as part of this journey. Now you can understand why Pete was behaving in such a way and why he'd felt the need to make a splash. Once this was clear, you took some time to explain your own personal goals and how things are in the team. You explained that you were plannning to start a family and were contemplating a career break. Once both of you understood the deeper personal issues, it became relatively simple to find

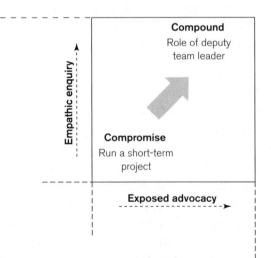

Figure 6.3 *Exposed advocacy, empathic enquiry*

an outcome that would be successful and sustainable (see Figure 6.3). You agree that Pete can, wherever possible, take greater responsibility for high-profile projects that come into the team. In return, you can reduce the amount of evening and weekend work that you were doing and spend time preparing the house for the new arrival. The original shared success could have worked but was not really satisfying and sustainable. The final solution is an agreement that satisfies real personal criteria.

Take it to the limit

The shift from compromise to compound success is based on your ability and desire to take the advocacy and enquiry dimensions to the limit.

If the relationship isn't reaching its full potential, are you really using the full power of exposed advocacy and empathic enquiry?

Is all your energy and passion focused on extracting from the other person their personal success criteria and helping them understand your own?

The highest level of interaction is one where the communication between groups of people results in compound outcomes and the amplification of people's ideas. As people expose their thoughts, ideas and personal patterns, so the level of understanding and knowledge within the room will expand. This type of approach needs to happen in scenario- or business-planning workshops, where the interaction between people will create new ideas, themes and patterns that might not have existed before the event. However, to ensure that the ideas are new from within the group and not just a compromise, there needs to be a concerted effort from all parties to focus on the give-and-take aspects within the relationships.

The V-ness factors

The ability to share success is often driven by the hidden factors in a relationship, the V-ness factors (see Figure 6.4). These are:

● the extent to which you share the same values and beliefs as the others in the relationship

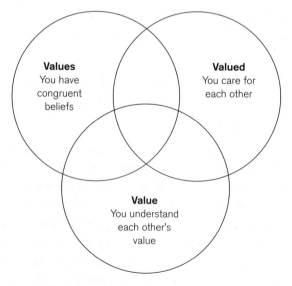

Values
You have congruent beliefs

Valued
You care for each other

Value
You understand each other's value

Figure 6.4   *Value, values, valued*

- the extent to which care and consideration are demonstrated, with the result that people feel valued

- the extent to which you demonstrate that you understand the value the other person adds to the relationship.

These three variables offer a significant contribution to the success of any relationship, and failure to deal with any of the factors limits the opportunity to share success.

Values

At the heart of any organization, family or social group are the values of the individuals who make up the culture. It's these personal and shared beliefs that bind people together or divide them, and generally make the world go round. We must therefore be sure that the values of the people, teams and organization are related in such a way as to facilitate success.

Espoused versus real values. People rarely take the time to appraise critically and understand what their values are and how they relate to the notion of shared success. Bear in mind that when considering people's values, though there might be visible clues, there are also many hidden facets and issues that can't be inferred from observation. This raises a number of important issues in relation to the use of values if we wish to share success:

- the values that people display may not be what they feel inside

- espoused values might not be the ones that drive the person or the organization

● the paradox of conforming to organizational values while aspiring to maintain one's own values can result in defence routines. This creates the falsification of behaviours and actions simply to satisfy the organization's social and political system.

Shared success can only be realized when there is alignment between the individual's and the organization's value set. It should be an overriding goal of any organization to discover and capture as much as possible of the value that is held within its people, and within this diversity of values should be positive discovery.

Cross the values bridge. We need to create a pincer movement to understand others' (friends', manager's, partner's, etc.) beliefs and values and to be prepared to offer our view of what we value and hold dear. No longer is it possible for the communication of company values to be a brainwashing process. The objective is to create a shared mindset, one that can help to create a common sense of resonance, even across diverse and varied value sets.

Bridge building is the crucial ability to manage the integration of what might be vastly differing value sets. Any political party wanting to move in a new direction has to take on board a new set of beliefs and values brought to the surface by the addition of new members. Initially conflict and confusion arise as members try to come to terms with a new set of norms and beliefs. Within this process people will generally ask two questions: which of my current beliefs will I concede to take on this new way of working? And, which of my core values should I retain as sacrosanct?

The values bridge (Figure 6.5) shows how you can manage different values by taking the value that someone else has espoused and mapping it with the values you hold important. To do this takes a degree of maturity because it's built on the principle that shared success can in many cases only be achieved by giving up certain strongly held beliefs and ideals. For each person you first need to understand what their values are, then prioritize them. Finally, the goal is to understand the other person's hierarchy of values and then build a bridge between the two value sets so that both understand those areas you're both prepared to concede, and to suggest clearly what isn't negotiable and can't be shifted.

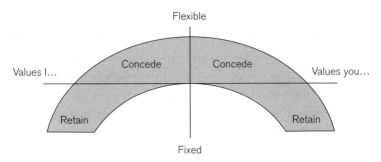

Figure 6.5   *Values I, values you*

Stretch the values bandwidth. Once you both understand the boundaries you're operating within, it's easier to manage the boundaries and start to accept and operate under someone else's value set. This approach is known as values bandwidth management (see Figure 6.6). The objective of this approach is to allow people to understand and adapt to each other's value sets within a managed framework. This means that value differences can be managed and provide a vehicle by which people can share success on their own terms.

Imagine two people who have started to work together on a new time-critical project. They get along well but realize they have quite differing views on the right and wrong way to work in a difficult situation. One of them might believe that when the chips are down then it's right to ignore the family commitments and focus entirely on work. The other person believes that work is only part of their life and has a personal commitment to be home at night to put the children to bed and read them a story. There is little chance that these two people will agree because of their entrenched and absolute beliefs. But it might be that they can identify some points of flex and operate in the concede area of bandwidth ('a' in Figure 6.6). It might turn out that they're both happy to work on Saturday morning in order to meet the tight deadline because this doesn't run counter to their beliefs and commitments. After some time and discussion they might move to bandwidth 'b' and realize that the trust fund is sufficiently high that they don't need to be in the office together to work on the project, so maybe they can work at home. Finally, they may move to bandwidth 'c' where they both respect and understand the other's values and are prepared to find shared success that will deliver the outcome without giving up their beliefs.

The most difficult aspect of the values bridge is the notion that you should concede in areas you hold dear. However, the goal is to be pragmatic, not submissive. I might decide that all my values are dear to me and that I'm not prepared to give up any of them – the chances that there might be someone in this life

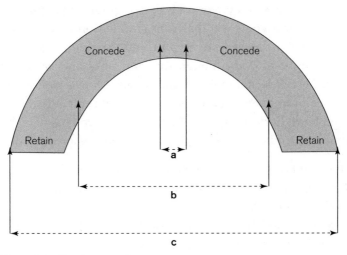

Figure 6.6 *Retain, concede*

who has a value set that exactly matches my own are low, and so there's every chance I'll die a sad and lonely old devil. It's right to have a set of core values that you hold on to and don't let go of no matter what, but it also makes sense to have a set that are important but negotiable.

To make the values bridge work you have to ask youself three questions:

- Do you know what your values are in priority order?

- Do you know others' values in priority order?

- To what extent are you prepared to give and take in order to achieve shared success?

I know of many situations where a failure to address these issues has resulted in problems for the individual and the company where they work. I met one group of people who worked for a company that was founded on a set of core values. These values were used to bind the group together as they grew and went though difficult times and each new recruit was selected to match the values. All was well until a change in leadership occurred and the values that had been lived by right from the outset changed. The end result is that almost an entire team left the business over a short period.

They felt that the company no longer understood the values that were important and non-negotiable to them and they had no choice but to leave. The use of the values bridge might not have prevented the mass departure, but it would have offered a vehicle by which people could talk about their feelings and how their personal priorities were being disregarded.

To what extent are you aware of your values and the values of the people you live and work with? To what extent do you discuss these values and how they affect your relationships? To what extent are you prepared to give way on your ideals and correspondingly require others to give way on theirs?

Valued

What is it that makes you give the best of yourself in a task? What is it that makes you go that extra mile to make a relationship work that bit better? What is it that makes you want to work with someone a second or third time even if the previous projects didn't quite deliver all that was expected? It's often because you feel that the person, team or organization appreciates you and the work you put into a task.

One simple example is that of a schoolteacher called Eric Watson. One day Eric received a phone call and the caller said: 'This is James Smith . . . you taught me at school 16 years ago. I'm in the area on holiday and knowing you lived around here thought I'd like to take you out to dinner.' Throughout the dinner Eric couldn't but wonder why James was wining and dining him. At the coffee stage he commented on the delightful meal and then came the answer. Rather shyly James said, 'I've got a very good job. I'm a mechanical engineer and it's all down to you. Your science lessons got me interested, not just because of the actual lesson, but your enthusiasm. Science lessons were the highlight of the day, and this is my way of saying thank you.' Eric reflected afterwards how he survives the constant problem of bullies, changing work schemes and new systems, and came to one conclusion: the old-fashioned occasional apple from a grateful pupil. In the same way that a teacher enjoys feeling valued by the children and the system, we all need to feel valued by the recipients of our efforts.

The smile that says a thousand words. If you've ever performed in a band, played sports for an audience, performed in a play or worked on a checkout till in the supermarket, you know how soul-destroying it can be to receive negative feedback or sometimes, even worse, no feedback. Often all it needs is one person to smile and say thank you, clap with enthusiasm or shout your name out with pride at the end of the performance to make it all worthwhile. People do better when they feel better, and people feel better when they're given positive feedback and personal reinforcement.

How often do you give positive feedback when people deserve it? Do you just assume they know they've done all right? It still amazes me just how often people go through a supermarket checkout without offering any warmth or feedback to the person stuck behind the till. This poor person is jammed in a space smaller than a stair cupboard, receiving low pay and dealing with all sorts of clientele, and yet nearly everyone I meet always has a smile and will help cheer up my day. It really jars when people walk through and can't be bothered to offer the smallest thank you or polite goodbye. Even worse is the pseudo 'Thank you' said with no link to the heart dimension. The only way to make people feel really valued for their efforts is to use all three dimensions, head, hand and heart. You have to know with your heart why you're saying thank you and use your whole body to demonstrate that it's a real and genuine, personal, 'Thank you'.

Just what is the cost of a thank you? How often do your manager, partner, colleagues or friends really make you feel valued for something you've done? Or, to look at that question another way: How often do you truly make other people feel valued for the effort they put into something for you? The picture your child painted for you, the extra hours overtime that your team member put in on a Saturday morning, or the fact that your partner brought you a coffee in bed – do you really make time to look for these efforts and read them with your heart? Or have you become oblivious to it all? Even as I write these words I think back on the times that I've been working in the office and one of the children has brought me a picture they'd painted for me. Though I often responded with a head and hand response, saying and doing the right things, in reality my heart was not involved in the interaction. I was still focused on the paper I was working on. The sad thing is, I can never have those moments again. They're lost – and that is such a waste. It's within the power of all of us to give strokes of recognition to those we want to feel valued.

It costs nothing but delivers rewards that seal relationships, and can help deliver sustainable shared success. Strokes are in essence a unit or statement of recognition. Some strokes are positive and some are negative. Some strokes are driven by the hand dimension. This might be a touch of thanks on the shoulder or a round of applause at the end of a presentation. Some might be head-based and driven by an intellectual recognition of effort. This might be an email to say thank you or a write-up in the in-house magazine. Others might be heart-based where you sit down with someone and tell them how you really feel about the effort they've made. Even when the strokes have a primary dimension, it's important that they contain some element of all three factors of head, hand and heart; without this the stroke will feel false and soulless.

There is a downside to this idea of valued strokes, and that is the 'professional thanker'. These are the people who have just been on a customer service course or a 'How to get the best from your people' programme. They arrive back home or in the office with a huge smile and full of a desire to reward everyone every time they do something, every minute of the day. No matter what you do they'll find a way to thank you for your efforts. They end up like the game show host smiling and loving everyone, but often underneath they're still the same old person. I don't wish to undervalue such programmes, but just make you aware. If someone's instinctive orientation isn't naturally to show how much they genuinely value you, just going on a course won't change their ingrained behaviour. It will change the hand, it might change the head, but, deep down, change to the heart takes longer and needs time and support to be sustainable.

Value

Consider the human instrument as something that interfaces with the world. As we interact with the environment we make different types of exchanges. We take in oxygen and give out carbon dioxide; we take in food and water and give out waste to be reprocessed; we take in information, process it, possibly add some value and then pass on that knowledge in return for some personal benefit.

We trade our personal capital as a form of soft currency. We pay money to read someone else's book and use this information to write a paper at work; we attend a course to gain parenting skills to help our children grow; or we pay to see a play that will give us insight into someone else's emotional view of the world, and use this experience to build a better relationship with a friend or colleague.

If we look at these examples, they fall into three currency groups: we exchange currency or value with the world in terms of how we think (head), act (hand) or feel (heart). In the vast majority of cases we draw on all three currencies to create value in the market. Although all three might be used to deliver a single product, it's likely that one of them will take a dominant role.

As a musician my dominant factor is a hand currency because my added value comes from the skills of playing the guitar. As an author the dominant factor is head currency because I am presenting you with my ideas and mental tools. Much of my market value as a consultant comes from the heart currency and my ability to create effective emotional relationships with my clients. This isn't to suggest that the people who watch me play in the local bar don't value my emotions as I play or my ability to know what notes to play. The core added value is around the capability to play the guitar, and the other currencies help position it in the market. When we consider all three areas, we can understand how we use the idea of head, hand and heart currencies to trade with the world.

Don't blame others for not recognizing your value. Think about some of the primary activities you undertake in your life – parent, schoolteacher, manager, sportsperson, and so on – where you have to produce a shared output with another person, team or organization. Take each one and consider its component parts in terms of head, hand and heart (see Figure 6.7).

For each element, think about the value you're contributing to others and consider whether you're satisfied that you're getting the rewards you deserve. The currency might be monetary if you're working for a company, or emotional thanks when you've done something for your partner or your child. If, in your actions, there's an imbalance between the three dimensions, and even though your intention is altruistic, it might be that you cherish the payment too much – that treasured smile from your partner or your child's simple thank you. If this is the case, and recognition is one of the

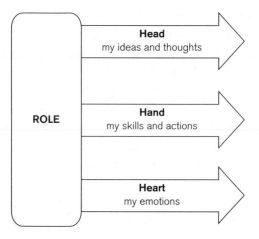

Figure 6.7 *Role*

primary motivators for you, performing acts of kindness and not necessarily getting what you feel is the right response will mean you develop inner tension or simply withdraw your efforts or favours because you feel uncomfortable and under-valued.

An obvious example of this is in a work situation. We've all been there. You've just spent hours and hours at home over the weekend trying to finish off a report or stayed behind at work for a while to tidy up the bench. When this isn't recognized by the company, it's irritating and leads to frustration and a withdrawal of work effort the next time you're called on to help out. But it's the type of reaction that limits your chance to share success because the frustration and anger will always come out in some form or another.

People often blame the company and bemoan the fact that their efforts haven't been recognized or valued. Rubbish! The onus is on you to map, measure, manage and market your personal value. It's not their responsibility to pamper and comfort you. It's your personal capital so it behoves you to place a value on it and ensure that you receive a fair and suitable reward from the market. This type of mentality is the same as a high street shop blaming the customers for not shopping with them. At the end of the day it's a question of supply and demand – you have products that the company needs: realize the value or find someone else who will. If you don't have products that the company needs now or in the future, get some! Or beware the next round of downsizing.

If you believe you're not receiving a fair and equitable reward for your effort, distraction and disquiet will set in and erode the sustainability of success.

Robert Louis Stevenson said, 'Everyone lives by selling something.' So, ask yourself: What do I trade with the world to create success? Do I determine its market value? Do others place the same value on my capital? This point is critical because imbalanced reward will limit any chances you have of repeating your successes.

V-ness imbalance

Some people are unable to share success, not because they don't use the ideas in the V-ness model, but because they have different preferences and strengths in each of the three areas.

For example a colleague of mine had a problem where a sudden change in V-ness balance caused her to rethink her position within a company and ultimately to leave. When she first joined the company, it was a small fledgling business that was driven by all three V-ness factors. Of the three factors, the roots of the business were founded in the core values but there was also a shared desire to earn a decent wage and maximize a return on their personal value in the market. Although the 'valued' factor was important as they often operated as free agents, their need for peer feedback and strokes of recognition was minimal because people were happy to pick up on this whenever they met for a social lunch or team meeting.

As the company started to grow at a rapid rate, it developed a strong brand in the market and reached a point where it had quadrupled in size. A new management team was formed with the goal of taking the business into a new phase of strategic and operational success. At this point the V-ness factor changed. The shift from a values-based culture moved toward a cost-based style of operating. From the senior team's point of view this made sense – so many new people meant they had to guarantee future income streams. However, for this person the values driver was still strong and something started to feel wrong. She couldn't necessarily explain what it was, but she knew that the level of her internal discomfort meant that it was time to leave.

This tale doesn't exist in isolation. We all know of other people who have become disillusioned, left the company, divorced, lost friends because of the same subtle shift in the V-ness balance. The main problem is when the shift is subtle or imperceptible. If a problem happens within an organization or relationship in an unambiguous way, the shift can be discussed openly and people can make choices about their future. When the shift takes place over time, it's not discussed in an open forum and deceit, bad feeling and apathy filter into the relationships.

The challenge for us all is to be sensitive to the balance of the V-ness factors. We need to be tuned into our preferences, the preferences of others and the environment in general. If there is an imbalance or conflict across our values, how we feel valued, and how we reward value, it must be understood so that the option to share success is managed and remains sustainable.

Share success – the three levels

Leader of leaders	**Lead leaders** – When leading other leaders one of the hardest battles to fight is how to manage the balance between letting leaders lead (and set their own direction) while ensuring that the necessary alignment is maintained across the group. This needs a special person who can balance out the need to let the leader run wild while understanding how greater gain comes from building and maintaining bridges within the system, thus creating a great strength – as with the strength that comes from intertwining of strands to create a rope.
Leader of others	**Lead others** – Understand that shared success delivers long-term sustainable results and avoids the drive for selfish outcome.
Leader of self	**Lead yourself** – Be prepared to enquire into other people's needs and don't focus just on presenting your own viewpoint and needs.

Share success: quick summary

1 Personal leadership that is selfish and short-lived is not true success. The only real form of personal leadership is one founded on the notion of shared outcomes and sustainable performance.

2 At the heart of your ability to share success is the need to understand and align the V-ness factors: values; feeling valued; and personal value.

3 The extent to which you feel valued by your partner, manager or company can make a huge difference in your willingness to give a little more.

4 The onus is on you to promote your value in the market and ensure that you receive a fair and equitable reward.

5 Unless you share values with other people or are willing to accept their values, any relationship will be short-lived.

6 You achieve a compound or collaborative relationship through two key behaviours: you must be able to find out and understand what success is for others; you must have the courage to advocate your needs so they understand what success is for you.

7 A combination of the ability to give your needs and get the other person's wishes from them can result in four types of success: squandered; subordinate; selfish; or shared.

epilogue

Oz, left to himself, smiled to think of his success in giving the Scarecrow and the Tinman and the Lion exactly what they thought they wanted. 'How can I help being a humbug,' he said, 'when all these people make me do things that everybody knows can't be done? It was easy to make the Scarecrow and the Lion and the Woodman happy, because they imagined I could do anything.'

The Wizard of Oz, L. Frank Baum

Personal leadership is just that – leading yourself. Don't be sucked into a belief that someone else can create a leadership solution for you. If you get this far in the book and agree that the core principles that underpin the need for personal leadership are right for you, the next thing to do is put the book away for a month. Go away and think about how you lead yourself and others; how you'd like to lead yourself and others; and what you might need to do to enhance this process. Then you can start to define where you're heading and how you'll get there in a way that fits your own map.

I wish you well on your journey.

Please feel free to email me on mick@mickcope.com or log on to the website at www.mickcope.com to let me know how you're getting on or to share your thoughts and feelings about the personal leadership framework.

further reading

Bailey, J., 'King of Karma predicts bright future', *Sunday Times*, 4 June 2000.

Battram, A. *Navigating Complexity, The Industrial Society*, 1996, p.104.

Bolman G. and T. Deal, *Reframing Organisations*, Jossey Bass, 1991, p.14.

Buchanan, D. and D. Body, *The Expertise of the Change Agent*, Prentice-Hall, London, 1992.

Hiscock, J., 'Vinnie plays it for real', *Daily Telegraph*, 25 July 2000.

Jones, H., 'Rodent or a rat bag?', *Financial Times*, 2 May 2000.

Meyerson, W. and S. Kramer, 'Trust and temporary groups', *Trust in Organisations*, p.184.

Murray, D., 'Ken orders transport chiefs out of the cars and on to the tube', *Evening Standard*, 6 August 2000.

Ridpath, M., *The Marketmaker*, Penguin, London, 1998, p.110.

Ross, D., 'A star on the horizon', *The Independent*, 7 August 2000.

Senge, P. *et al.*, *The Dance of Change*, Nicholas Brealey Publishing, London, 1999, p.5.

Sims H. and P. Lorenzi, *The New Leadership Paradigm*, Sage Publications, USA, 1992, p.272.

Watson, E., 'How one phone call made up for 40 years of classroom war', *Mail On Sunday*, 6 August 2000.

Zand, D., 'Trust and managerial problem solving', *Administrative Science Quarterly*.

What am I learning:

Chapter 1 : Choose your choice

- It is important to keep control of your choices otherwise you will allow other/external factor control your life

Chapter 2 : Know where you are heady

- Understand what you really want and base your goals/actions on these.
- By focussing on where you are going you will be able to get through all the distractions that you will face.
- Don't confuse who you are with what you do or own.
- What is my personal mission statement
- What are my core values?